Buried Child

&

Seduced

&

Suicide In B$^\flat$

Sam Shepard

Other Plays by Sam Shepard

Action
Angel City
Back Bog Beast Bait
Chicago
Cowboy Mouth
Cowboys #2
Curse of the Starving Class
Forensic and the Navigator
Fourteen Hundred Thousand
Geography of a Horsedreamer
The Holy Ghostly
Icarus's Mother
Killer's Head
La Turista
The Mad Dog Blues
Melodrama Play
Operation Sidewinder
Red Cross
The Rock Garden
The Tooth of Crime
The Unseen Hand

Buried Child

&

Seduced

&

Suicide In B$^{\flat}$

Sam Shepard

Urizen Books

Printed in the United States of America

ISBN 0–89396–010–1 (cloth)
0–89396–011–X (paper)

Urizen Books, Inc.
66 West Broadway
New York 10007

Library of Congress Catalog Card Number 79-66031

Contents

For Joe Chaikin

Introduction

By Jack Richardson

"What difference does it make? It's a good story. One story's as good as another. It's all in the way you tell it. That's what counts. That's what makes the difference."

Thus speaks Henry Hackamore, the Howard Hughes-like recluse in the play *Seduced*, and these lines could very well make up the motto for the three Sam Shepard plays collected in this volume. For the characters we meet in these works are all searching for suitable stories for themselves, seeking special histories that might explain who they are and how they came to be that way. Their pasts have gaps and horrors that must somehow be filled in or exorcised with words; their present is a maze of disjointed moments, seemingly random behavior, and crossed monologues; their future, that point toward which the action of the plays directs them, filled with a menacing ambivalence. Caught in a world of random action and shifting identities, finding the right story and the proper mode in which to tell it becomes for these characters, as well as for the playwright who creates them, a means of making up a world that is both personal and habitable.

Of course, the above description suits the personae of a good many modern plays. From Surrealists, through Beckett, and on to epigoni like Pinter and Orton, runs a tradition of dramatic behavior that lies outside the brackets of conventional realism. The accepted morality plays of our time are concerned with removing the conventions of coherence in which we lead our lives and in finding ways to insinuate and symbolize what is left once the protective covering has been stripped away.

Now this method is easy to abuse. Every year dozens of plays try to impress us with the discovery that life is not a well-joined, reasonable enterprise. The allegorical action, the sets in limbo, the dialogue of non-sequiturs, the eccentric manner, the unexpected lyrical effusion—these are now the stock-in-trade of every second-rate playwright out to discomfort his audience with a big unpleasant truth about life.

But what are clichéd routines in inferior hands, become, when used by a real dramatist like Shepard, an apposite and vital technique. No matter how antic or askew the action of his plays or the attitudes of his characters, one never feels that things have been arranged for the sake of a metaphysical point or to diffuse an atmosphere of facile theatrical mystery. Somehow, Shepard manages to strike a balance between naturalistic detail and the wilder, more secret landscapes of being. He has found a way of maintaining a tension between the banal and the strange that gives his plays the quality of lucid dreams. He makes us believe in the unexpected because he conjures it out of very ordinary things, building slowly the mood of his plays upon a foundation of sharply formed images and precisely observed human habits. Like all good dramatists he knows how to shape his characters into acceptable exaggerations of life, to earn for them the right to lyrical moments and extraordinary actions.

Shepard is able to stretch the imagination of his audience to such lengths because he has found a language that serves equally well as a vehicle for the antic or the ordinary. In *Buried Child*, for example, the figures of everyday speech—the bromides, exclamations, and metaphors of middle American life—are arranged in such a way that they take on a fresh, almost frantic meaning. Characters reach exquisite moments of bafflement and mutual misunderstanding without ever abandoning the flat tones of ordinary banter. In *Seduced*, Shepard moves to a different level of diction, matching the ornate, imagistic language of his main character against the slangy, empty-headed speech of those around him; and in *Suicide in B♭*, we have several virtuoso performances of rhetoric, long musical solos in speech that improvise their way through the rapid changes of the play's action. Yet, through all its permutations, Shepard's dialogue always maintains its affiliation with reality, with the concrete and the homespun. Consequently, no matter how strange the events in which his characters are caught, they become imbued with a palpable actuality. Language appropriates them, brings them down to earth, and makes them appear natural and comprehensible.

Shepard's use of dialogue makes his work especially readable. Even if he did not provide us in his stage directions with careful descriptions of the settings and characters of his plays, we would know enough about them from the speeches on the page to form a clear idea in our minds about the world we were in and the people who inhabited it. Take Halie's speech about the merits of her dead son in *Buried Child*. After only a few lines, she really needs no actress for her embodiment:

Of course, he'd still be alive today if he hadn't married into the Catholics. The Mob... Catholic women are the devil incarnate. He wouldn't listen. Blind. I knew. Everyone knew. The wedding was more like a funeral. You remember? All those Italians. All that horrible black, greasy hair. The smell of cheap cologne. I think even the priest was wearing a pistol.

And this reminiscence of Henry Hackamore in *Seduced* evokes the very lineaments and sound of the man:

...It's the same thing I saw in Texas when I was a boy. The same thing I've always seen. I saw myself. Alone. Standing in open country. Flat, barren. Wasted....As though men were a joke in the face of it. I heard rattlesnakes laughing. Coyotes. Cactus stabbing the blue air. Miles of heat and wind and red rock where nothing grew but the sand. And far off, invisible little men were huddled against it in cities. In tiny towns. In organizations....Sad demented little morons moving in circles.

It is not only the set speeches of characters that make these plays rewarding to read. Shepard's way with the short, interacting lines of dialogue keeps one always aware of the mood and rhythm of a scene, so that one can easily grasp and enjoy the play's overall dramatic tempo.

Now although I have emphasized the verbal excellence of these works—an emphasis understandable when plays are to be read instead of seen—it would be a disservice to them to leave the impression that they are only bright exercises in eloquence. Shepard's works also possess a very cogent meaning, and make sense in ways other than aesthetic. His vision of America's myths and rituals, of our dreams of power and of family love, of our pioneer history of drift and disconnection, of our art and political manners, is sharply and brutally observed. It is a vision shaped, as all real art is, in a very personal way, but it is a vision that is accessible to anyone with the patience to listen carefully to another's voice.

The voice in which Shepard addresses us is filled with many recognizable accents from our past and present. It is a very American voice, well-suited to tell strange and extravagant stories in a way that beguiles our disbelief and it is a voice unique in our theater.

BURIED CHILD

Pulitzer Prize 1979

While the rain of your fingertips falls,
while the rain of your bones falls,
and your laughter and marrow fall down,
you come flying.

Pablo Neruda

CHARACTERS:

DODGE–In his seventies.

HALIE–His wife. Mid-sixties.

TILDEN–Their oldest son.

BRADLEY–Their next oldest son, an amputee.

VINCE–Tilden's son.

SHELLY–Vince's girl friend.

FATHER DEWIS–A Protestant minister

Buried Child was first produced at the Magic Theatre, San Francisco, on June 27, 1978. It was directed by Robert Woodruff with the following cast:

> Dodge: Joseph Gistirak
> Halie: Catherine Willis
> Tilden: Dennis Ludlow
> Bradley: William M. Carr
> Shelly: Betsy Scott
> Vince: Barry Lane
> Father Dewis: Rj Frank

The New York premiere was directed by Robert Woodruff with the following cast:

> Dodge: Richard Hamilton
> Halie: Jacqueline Brookes
> Tilden: Tom Noonan
> Bradley: Jay O. Sanders
> Shelly: Mary McDonnell
> Vince: Christopher McCann
> Father Dewis: Bill Wiley

ACT 1

SCENE:

Day. Old wooden staircase down left with pale, frayed carpet laid down on the steps. The stairs lead off stage left up into the wings with no landing. Up right is an old, dark green sofa with the stuffing coming out in spots. Stage right of the sofa is an upright lamp with a faded yellow shade and a small night table with several small bottles of pills on it. Down right of the sofa, with the screen facing the sofa, is a large, old-fashioned brown T.V.. A flickering blue light comes from the screen, but no image, no sound. In the dark, the light of the lamp and the T.V. slowly brighten in the black space. The space behind the sofa, upstage, is a large, screened-in porch with a board floor. A solid interior door to stage right of the sofa, leading into the room on stage; and another screen door up left, leading from the porch to the outside. Beyond that are the shapes of dark elm trees.

Gradually the form of DODGE *is made out, sitting on the couch, facing the T.V., the blue light flickering on his face. He wears a well-worn T-shirt, suspenders, khaki work pants and brown slippers. He's covered himself in an old brown blanket. He's very thin and sickly looking, in his late seventies. He just stares at the T.V.. More light fills the stage softly. The sound of light rain.* DODGE *slowly tilts his head back and stares at the ceiling for a while, listening to the rain. He lowers his head again and stares at the T.V.. He turns his head slowly to the left and stares at the cushion of the sofa next to the one he's sitting on. He pulls his left arm out from under the blanket, slides his hand under the cushion, and pulls out a bottle of whiskey. He looks down left toward the staircase, listens, then uncaps the bottle, takes a long swig and caps it again. He puts the bottle back under the cushion and stares at the T.V. He starts to cough slowly and softly. The coughing gradually builds. He holds one hand to his mouth and tries to stifle it. The coughing gets louder, then suddenly stops when he hears the sound of his wife's voice coming from the top of the staircase.*

HALIE'S VOICE: Dodge?

DODGE *just stares at the T.V. Long pause. He stifles two short coughs.*

HALIE'S VOICE: Dodge! You want a pill, Dodge?
He doesn't answer. Takes the bottle out again and takes another long swig. Puts the bottle back stares at T.V., pulls blanket up around his neck.
HALIE'S VOICE: You know what it is, don't you? It's the rain! Weather. That's it. Every time. Every time you get like this, it's the rain. No sooner does the rain start then you start. *(pause)* Dodge?
He makes no reply. Pulls a pack of cigarettes out from his sweater and lights one. Stares at T.V. pause.
HALIE'S VOICE: You should see it coming down up here. Just coming down in sheets. Blue sheets. The bridge is pretty near flooded. What's it like down there? Dodge?
DODGE *turns his head back over his left shoulder and takes a look out through the porch. He turns back to the T.V.*
DODGE: *(to himself)* Catastrophic.
HALIE'S VOICE: What? What'd you say, Dodge?
DODGE: *(louder)* It looks like rain to me! Plain old rain!
HALIE'S VOICE: Rain? Of course it's rain! Are you having a seizure or something! Dodge? *(pause)* I'm coming down there in about five minutes if you don't answer me!
DODGE: Don't come down.
HALIE'S VOICE: What!
DODGE: *(louder)* Don't come down!
He has another coughing attack. Stops.
HALIE'S VOICE: You should take a pill for that! I don't see why you just don't take a pill. Be done with it once and for all. Put a stop to it.
He takes bottle out again. Another swig. Returns bottle.
HALIE'S VOICE: It's not Christian, but it works. It's not necessarily Christian, that is. We don't know. There's some things the ministers can't even answer. I, personally, can't see anything wrong with it. Pain is pain. Pure and simple. Suffering is a different matter. That's entirely different. A pill seems as good an answer as any. Dodge? *(pause)* Dodge, are you watching baseball?
DODGE: No.
HALIE'S VOICE: What?
DODGE: *(louder)* No!
HALIE'S VOICE: What're you watching? You shouldn't be watching anything that'll get you excited! No horse racing!
DODGE: They don't race on Sundays.

HALIE'S VOICE: What?

DODGE: *(louder)* They don't race on Sundays!

HALIE'S VOICE: Well they shouldn't race on Sundays.

DODGE: Well they don't!

HALIE'S VOICE: Good. I'm amazed they still have that kind of legislation. That's amazing.

DODGE: Yeah, it's amazing.

HALIE'S VOICE: What?

DODGE: *(louder)* It is amazing!

HALIE'S VOICE: It is. It truly is. I would've thought these days they'd be racing on Christmas even. A big flashing Christmas tree right down at the finish line.

DODGE: *(shakes his head)* No.

HALIE'S VOICE: They used to race on New Year's! I remember that.

DODGE: They never raced on New Year's!

HALIE'S VOICE: Sometimes they did.

DODGE: They never did!

HALIE'S VOICE: Before we were married they did!

DODGE *waves his hand in disgust at the staircase. Leans back in sofa. Stares at T.V.*

HALIE'S VOICE: I went once. With a man.

DODGE: *(mimicking her)* Oh, a "man."

HALIE'S VOICE: What?

DODGE: Nothing!

HALIE'S VOICE: A wonderful man. A breeder.

DODGE: A what?

HALIE'S VOICE: A breeder! A horse breeder! Thoroughbreds.

DODGE: Oh, Thoroughbreds. Wonderful.

HALIE'S VOICE: That's right. He knew everything there was to know.

DODGE: I bet he taught you a thing or two huh? Gave you a good turn around the old stable!

HALIE'S VOICE: Knew everything there was to know about horses. We won bookoos of money that day.

DODGE: What?

HALIE'S VOICE: Money! We won every race I think.

DODGE: Bookoos?

HALIE'S VOICE: Every single race.

DODGE: Bookoos of money?

HALIE'S VOICE: It was one of those kind of days.

DODGE: New Year's!

HALIE'S VOICE: Yes! It might've been Florida. Or California! One of those two.

DODGE: Can I take my pick?

HALIE'S VOICE: It was Florida!

DODGE: Aha!

HALIE'S VOICE: Wonderful! Absolutely wonderful! The sun was just gleaming. Flamingos. Bougainvilleas. Palm trees.

DODGE: *(to himself, mimicking her)* Bougainvilleas. Palm trees.

HALIE'S VOICE: Everything was dancing with life! There were all kinds of people from everywhere. Everyone was dressed to the nines. Not like today. Not like they dress today.

DODGE: When was this anyway?

HALIE'S VOICE: This was long before I knew you.

DODGE: Must've been.

HALIE'S VOICE: Long before. I was escorted.

DODGE: To Florida?

HALIE'S VOICE: Yes. Or it might've been California. I'm not sure which.

DODGE: All that way you were escorted?

HALIE'S VOICE: Yes.

DODGE: And he never laid a finger on you I suppose? *(long silence)* Halie?

No answer. Long pause.

HALIE'S VOICE: Are you going out today?

DODGE: *(gesturing toward rain)* In this?

HALIE'S VOICE: I'm just asking a simple question.

DODGE: I rarely go out in the bright sunshine, why would I go out in this?

HALIE'S VOICE: I'm just asking because I'm not doing any shopping today. And if you need anything you should ask Tilden.

DODGE: Tilden's not here!

HALIE'S VOICE: He's in the kitchen.

DODGE *looks toward stage left, then back toward T.V.*

DODGE: All right.

HALIE'S VOICE: What?

DODGE: *(louder)* All right!

HALIE'S VOICE: Don't scream. It'll only get your coughing started.

DODGE: All right.

HALIE'S VOICE: Just tell Tilden what you want and he'll get it. *(pause)* Bradley should be over later.

DODGE: Bradley?

HALIE'S VOICE: Yes. To cut your hair.

DODGE: My hair? I don't need my hair cut!

HALIE'S VOICE: It won't hurt!

DODGE: I don't need it!

HALIE'S VOICE: It's been more than two weeks Dodge.

DODGE: I don't need it!

HALIE'S VOICE: I have to meet Father Dewis for lunch.

DODGE: You tell Bradley that if he shows up here with those clippers, I'll kill him!

HALIE'S VOICE: I won't be very late. No later than four at the very latest.

DODGE: You tell him! Last time he left me almost bald! And I wasn't even awake! I was sleeping! I woke up and he'd already left!

HALIE'S VOICE: That's not my fault!

DODGE: You put him up to it!

HALIE'S VOICE: I never did!

DODGE: You did too! You had some fancy, stupid meeting planned! Time to dress up the corpse for company! Lower the ears a little! Put up a little front! Surprised you didn't tape a pipe to my mouth while you were at it! That woulda' looked nice! Huh? A pipe? Maybe a bowler hat! Maybe a copy of the Wall Street Journal casually placed on my lap!

HALIE'S VOICE: You always imagine the worst things of people!

DODGE: That's not the worst! That's the least of the worst!

HALIE'S VOICE: I don't need to hear it! All day long I hear things like that and I don't need to hear more.

DODGE: You better tell him!

HALIE'S VOICE: You tell him yourself! He's your own son. You should be able to talk to your own son.

DODGE: Not while I'm sleeping! He cut my hair while I was sleeping!

HALIE'S VOICE: Well he won't do it again.

DODGE: There's no guarantee.

HALIE'S VOICE: I promise he won't do it without your consent.

DODGE: *(after pause)* There's no reason for him to even come over here.

HALIE'S VOICE: He feels responsible.

DODGE: For my hair?

HALIE'S VOICE: For your appearance.

DODGE: My appearance is out of his domain! It's even out of mine! In fact, it's disappeared! I'm an invisible man!

HALIE'S VOICE: Don't be ridiculous.

DODGE: He better not try it. That's all I've got to say.

HALIE'S VOICE: Tilden will watch out for you.

DODGE: Tilden won't protect me from Bradley!

HALIE'S VOICE: Tilden's the oldest. He'll protect you.

DODGE: Tilden can't even protect himself!

HALIE'S VOICE: Not so loud! He'll hear you. He's right in the kitchen.

DODGE: *(yelling off left)* Tilden!

HALIE'S VOICE: Dodge, what are you trying to do?

DODGE: *(yelling off left)* Tilden, get in here!

HALIE'S VOICE: Why do you enjoy stirring things up?

DODGE: I don't enjoy anything!

HALIE'S VOICE: That's a terrible thing to say.

DODGE: Tilden!

HALIE'S VOICE: That's the kind of statement that leads people right to the end of their rope.

DODGE: Tilden!

HALIE'S VOICE: It's no wonder people turn to Christ!

DODGE: TILDEN!!

HALIE'S VOICE: It's no wonder the messengers of God's word are shouted down in public places!

DODGE: TILDEN!!!!

DODGE *goes into a violent, spasmodic coughing attack as* TILDEN *enters from stage left, his arms loaded with fresh ears of corn.* TILDEN *is* DODGE'S *oldest son, late forties, wears heavy construction boots, covered with mud, dark green work pants, a plaid shirt and a faded brown windbreaker. He has a butch haircut, wet from the rain. Something about him is profoundly burned out and displaced. He stops center stage with the ears of corn in his arms and just stares at Dodge until he slowly finishes his coughing attack.* DODGE *looks up at him slowly. He stares at the corn. Long pause as they watch each other.*

HALIE'S VOICE: Dodge, if you don't take that pill nobody's going to force you.

The two men ignore the voice.

DODGE: *(to* TILDEN*)* Where'd you get that?

TILDEN: Picked it.

DODGE: You picked all that?

TILDEN nods.

DODGE: You expecting company?

TILDEN: No.

DODGE: Where'd you pick it from?

TILDEN: Right out back.

DODGE: Out back where!

TILDEN: Right out in back.

DODGE: There's nothing out there!

TILDEN: There's corn.

DODGE: There hasn't been corn out there since about nineteen thirty five! That's the last time I planted corn out there!

TILDEN: It's out there now.

DODGE: *(yelling at stairs)* Halie!

HALIE'S VOICE: Yes dear!

DODGE: Tilden's brought a whole bunch of corn in here! There's no corn out in back is there?

TILDEN: *(to himself)* There's tons of corn.

HALIE'S VOICE: Not that I know of!

DODGE: That's what I thought.

HALIE'S VOICE: Not since about nineteen thirty five!

DODGE: *(to TILDEN)* That's right. Nineteen thirty five.

TILDEN: It's out there now.

DODGE: You go and take that corn back to wherever you got it from!

TILDEN: *(After pause, staring at DODGE)* It's picked. I picked it all in the rain. Once it's picked you can't put it back.

DODGE: I haven't had trouble with neighbors here for fifty-seven years. I don't even know who the neighbors are! And I don't wanna know! Now go put that corn back where it came from!

TILDEN *stares at* DODGE *then walks slowly over to him and dumps all the corn on* DODGE'S *lap and steps back.* DODGE *stares at the corn then back to* TILDEN. *Long pause.*

DODGE: Are you having trouble here, Tilden? Are you in some kind of trouble?

TILDEN: I'm not in any trouble.

DODGE: You can tell me if you are. I'm still your father.

TILDEN: I know you're still my father.

DODGE: I know you had a little trouble back in New Mexico. That's why you came out here.

TILDEN: I never had any trouble.

DODGE: Tilden, your mother told me all about it.

TILDEN: What'd she tell you?

TILDEN *pulls some chewing tobacco out of his jacket and bites off a plug.*

DODGE: I don't have to repeat what she told me! She told me all about it!

TILDEN: Can I bring my chair in from the kitchen?

DODGE: What?

TILDEN: Can I bring in my chair from the kitchen?

DODGE: Sure. Bring your chair in.

TILDEN *exits left.* DODGE *pushes all the corn off his lap onto the floor. He pulls the blanket off angrily and tosses it at one end of the sofa, pulls out the bottle and takes another swig.* TILDEN *enters again from left with a milking stool and a pail.* DODGE *hides the bottle quickly under the cushion before Tilden sees it.* TILDEN *sets the stool down by the sofa, sits on it, puts the pail in front of him on the floor.* TILDEN *starts picking up the ears of corn one at a time and husking them. He throws the husks and silk in the center of the stage and drops the ears into the pail each time he cleans one. He repeats this process as they talk.*

DODGE: *(after pause)* Sure is nice looking corn.

TILDEN: It's the best.

DODGE: Hybrid?

TILDEN: What?

DODGE: Some kinda fancy hybrid?

TILDEN: You planted it. I don't know what it is.

DODGE: *(pause)* Tilden, look, you can't stay here forever. You know that, don't you?

TILDEN: *(spits in spittoon)* I'm not.

DODGE: I know you're not. I'm not worried about that. That's not the reason I brought it up.

TILDEN: What's the reason?

DODGE: The reason is I'm wondering what you're gonna do.

TILDEN: You're not worried about me, are you?

DODGE: I'm not worried about you.

TILDEN: You weren't worried about me when I wasn't here. When I was in New Mexico.

DODGE: No, I wasn't worried about you then either.

TILDEN: You shoulda worried about me then.

DODGE: Why's that? You didn't do anything down there, did you?

TILDEN: I didn't do anything.

DODGE: Then why should I have worried about you?

TILDEN: Because I was lonely.

DODGE: Because you were lonely?

TILDEN: Yeah. I was more lonely than I've ever been before.

DODGE: Why was that?

TILDEN: *(pause)* Could I have some of that whiskey you've got?

DODGE: What whiskey? I haven't got any whiskey.

TILDEN: You've got some under the sofa.

DODGE: I haven't got anything under the sofa! Now mind your own damn business! Jesus God, you come into the house outa the middle of nowhere, haven't heard or seen you in twenty years and suddenly you're making accusations.

TILDEN: I'm not making accusations.

DODGE: You're accusing me of hoarding whiskey under the sofa!

TILDEN: I'm not accusing you.

DODGE: You just got through telling me I had whiskey under the sofa!

HALIE'S VOICE: Dodge?

DODGE: *(to* TILDEN*)* Now she knows about it!

TILDEN: She doesn't know about it.

HALIE'S VOICE: Dodge, are you talking to yourself down there?

DODGE: I'm talking to Tilden!

HALIE'S VOICE: Tilden's down there?

DODGE: He's right here!

HALIE'S VOICE: What?

DODGE: *(louder)* He's right here!

HALIE'S VOICE: What's he doing?

DODGE: *(to* TILDEN*)* Don't answer her.

TILDEN: *(to* DODGE*)* I'm not doing anything wrong.

DODGE: I know you're not.

HALIE'S VOICE: What's he doing down there!

DODGE: *(to* TILDEN*)* Don't answer.

TILDEN: I'm not.

HALIE'S VOICE: Dodge!

The men sit in silence. DODGE *lights a cigarette.* TILDEN *keeps husking corn, spits tobacco now and then in spittoon.*

HALIE'S VOICE: Dodge! He's not drinking anything, is he? You see to it that he doesn't drink anything! You've gotta watch out for him. It's our responsibility. He can't look after himself anymore, so we have to do it. Nobody else will do it. We can't just send him away somewhere. If we had lots of money we could send him away. But we don't. We never will. That's why we have to stay healthy. You and me. Nobody's going to look after us. Bradley can't look after us. Bradley can hardly look after himself. I was always hoping that Tilden would look out for Bradley when they got older. After Bradley lost his leg. Tilden's the oldest. I always thought he'd be the one to take responsibility. I had no idea in the world that Tilden would be so much trouble. Who would've dreamed. Tilden was an All-American, don't forget. Don't forget that. Fullback. Or quarterback. I forget which.

TILDEN: *(to himself)* Fullback. *(still husking)*

HALIE'S VOICE: Then when Tilden turned out to be so much trouble, I put all my hopes on Ansel. Of course Ansel wasn't as handsome, but he was smart. He was the smartest probably. I think he probably was. Smarter than Bradley, that's for sure. Didn't go and chop his leg off with a chain saw. Smart enough not to go and do that. I think he was smarter than Tilden too. Especially after Tilden got in all that trouble. Doesn't take brains to go to jail. Anybody knows that. Course then when Ansel died that left us all alone. Same as being alone. No different. Same as if they'd all died. He was the smartest. He could've earned lots of money. Lots and lots of money.

HALIE *enters slowly from the top of the staircase as she continues talking. Just her feet are seen at first as she makes her way down the stairs, a step at a time. She appears dressed completely in black, as though in mourning. Black handbag, hat with a veil, and pulling on elbow length black gloves. She is about sixty-five with pure white hair. She remains absorbed in what she's saying as she descends the stairs and doesn't really notice the two men who continue sitting there as they were before she came down, smoking and husking.*

HALIE: He would've took care of us, too. He would've seen to it that we were repaid. He was like that. He was a hero. Don't forget that. A genuine hero. Brave. Strong. And very intelligent. Ansel could've been a great man. One of the greatest. I only regret that he didn't die in action. It's not fitting for a man like that to die in a motel room. A soldier. He could've won a medal. He could've been decorated for valor. I've talked to Father Dewis about putting up a plaque for Ansel.

He thinks it's a good idea. He agrees. He knew Ansel when he used to play basketball. Went to every game. Ansel was his favorite player. He even recommended to the City Council that they put up a statue of Ansel. A big, tall statue with a basketball in one hand and a rifle in the other. That's how much he thinks of Ansel.

HALIE *reaches the stage and begins to wander around, still absorbed in pulling on her gloves, brushing lint off her dress and continuously talking to herself as the men just sit.*

HALIE: Of course, he'd still be alive today if he hadn't married into the Catholics. The Mob. How in the world he never opened his eyes to that is beyond me. Just beyond me. Everyone around him could see the truth. Even Tilden. Tilden told him time and again. Catholic women are the Devil incarnate. He wouldn't listen. He was blind with love. Blind. I knew. Everyone knew. The wedding was more like a funeral. You remember? All those Italians. All that horrible black, greasy hair. The smell of cheap cologne. I think even the priest was wearing a pistol. When he gave her the ring I knew he was a dead man. I knew it. As soon as he gave her the ring. But then it was the honeymoon that killed him. The honeymoon. I knew he'd never come back from the honeymoon. I kissed him and he felt like a corpse. All white. Cold. Icy blue lips. He never used to kiss like that. Never before. I knew then that she'd cursed him. Taken his soul. I saw it in her eyes. She smiled at me with that Catholic sneer of hers. She told me with her eyes that she'd murder him in his bed. Murder my son. She told me. And there was nothing I could do. Absolutely nothing. He was going with her, thinking he was free. Thinking it was love. What could I do? I couldn't tell him she was a witch. I couldn't tell him that. He'd have turned on me. Hated me. I couldn't stand him hating me and then dying before he ever saw me again. Hating me in his death bed. Hating me and loving her! How could I do that? I had to let him go. I had to. I watched him leave. I watched him throw gardenias as he helped her into the limousine. I watched his face disappear behind the glass.

She stops abruptly and stares at the corn husks. She looks around the space as though just waking up. She turns and looks hard at TILDEN *and* DODGE *who continue sitting calmly. She looks again at the corn husks.*

HALIE: *(pointing to the husks)* What's this in my house! *(kicks husks)* What's all this!

TILDEN *stops husking and stares at her.*

HALIE: *(to* DODGE*)* And you encourage him!

DODGE *pulls blanket over him again.*

DODGE: You're going out in the rain?

HALIE: It's not raining.

TILDEN *starts husking again.*

DODGE: Not in Florida it's not.

HALIE: We're not in Florida!

DODGE: It's not raining at the race track.

HALIE: Have you been taking those pills? Those pills always make you talk crazy. Tilden, has he been taking those pills?

TILDEN: He hasn't took anything.

HALIE: *(to* DODGE*)* What've you been taking?

DODGE: It's not raining in California or Florida or the race track. Only in Illinois. This is the only place it's raining. All over the rest of the world it's bright golden sunshine.

HALIE *goes to the night table next to the sofa and checks the bottle of pills.*

HALIE: Which ones did you take? Tilden, you must've seen him take something.

TILDEN: He never took a thing.

HALIE: Then why's he talking crazy?

TILDEN: I've been here the whole time.

HALIE: Then you've both been taking something!

TILDEN: I've just been husking the corn.

HALIE: Where'd you get that corn anyway? Why is the house suddenly full of corn?

DODGE: Bumper crop!

HALIE: *(moving center)* We haven't had corn here for over thirty years.

TILDEN: The whole back lot's full of corn. Far as the eye can see.

DODGE: *(to* HALIE*)* Things keep happening while you're upstairs, ya know. The world doesn't stop just because you're upstairs. Corn keeps growing. Rain keeps raining.

HALIE: I'm not unaware of the world around me! Thank you very much. It so happens that I have an over-all view from the upstairs. The back yard's in plain view of my window. And there's no corn to speak of. Absolutely none!

DODGE: Tilden wouldn't lie. If he says there's corn, there's corn.

HALIE: What's the meaning of this corn Tilden!

TILDEN: It's a mystery to me. I was out in back there. And the rain was coming down. And I didn't feel like coming back inside. I didn't feel the cold so much. I didn't mind the wet. So I was just walking. I was muddy but I didn't mind the mud so much. And I looked up. And I saw this stand of corn. In fact I was standing in it. So, I was standing in it.

HALIE: There isn't any corn outside Tilden! There's no corn! Now, you must've either stolen this corn or you bought it.

DODGE: He doesn't have any money.

HALIE: *(to* TILDEN*)* So you stole it!

TILDEN: I didn't steal it. I don't want to get kicked out of Illinois. I was kicked out of New Mexico and I don't want to get kicked out of Illinois.

HALIE: You're going to get kicked out of this house, Tilden, if you don't tell me where you got that corn!

TILDEN *starts crying softly to himself but keeps husking corn. Pause.*

DODGE: *(to* HALIE*)* Why'd you have to tell him that? Who cares where he got the corn? Why'd you have to go and tell him that?

HALIE: *(to* DODGE*)* It's your fault you know! You're the one that's behind all this! I suppose you thought it'd be funny! Some joke! Cover the house with corn husks. You better get this cleaned up before Bradley sees it.

DODGE: Bradley's not getting in the front door!

HALIE: *(kicking husks, striding back and forth)* Bradley's going to be very upset when he sees this. He doesn't like to see the house in disarray. He can't stand it when one thing is out of place. The slightest thing. You know how he gets.

DODGE: Bradley doesn't even live here!

HALIE: It's his home as much as ours. He was born in this house!

DODGE: He was born in a hog wallow.

HALIE: Don't you say that! Don't you ever say that!

DODGE: He was born in a goddamn hog wallow! That's where he was born and that's where he belongs! He doesn't belong in this house!

HALIE: *(she stops)* I don't know what's come over you, Dodge. I don't know what in the world's come over you. You've become an evil man. You used to be a good man.

DODGE: Six of one, a half dozen of another.

HALIE: You sit here day and night, festering away! Decomposing! Smelling up the house with your putrid body! Hacking your head off til all hours of the morning! Thinking up mean, evil, stupid things to say about your own flesh and blood!

DODGE: He's not my flesh and blood! My flesh and blood's buried in the back yard!

They freeze. Long pause. The men stare at her.

HALIE: *(quietly)* That's enough, Dodge. That's quite enough. I'm going out now. I'm going to have lunch with Father Dewis. I'm going to ask him about a monument. A statue. At least a plaque.

She crosses to the door up right. She stops.

HALIE: If you need anything, ask Tilden. He's the oldest. I've left some money on the kitchen table.

DODGE: I don't need anything.

HALIE: No, I suppose not. *(she opens the door and looks out through porch)* Still raining. I love the smell just after it stops. The ground. I won't be too late.

She goes out door and closes it. She's still visible on the porch as she crosses toward stage left screen door. She stops in the middle of the porch, speaks to DODGE *but doesn't turn to him.*

HALIE: Dodge, tell Tilden not to go out in the back lot anymore. I don't want him back there in the rain.

DODGE: You tell him. He's sitting right here.

HALIE: He never listens to me Dodge. He's never listened to me in the past.

DODGE: I'll tell him.

HALIE: We have to watch him just like we used to now. Just like we always have. He's still a child.

DODGE: I'll watch him.

HALIE: Good.

She crosses to screen door, left, takes an umbrella off a hook and goes out the door. The door slams behind her. Long pause. TILDEN *husks corn, stares at pail.* DODGE *lights a cigarette, stares at T.V.*

TILDEN: *(still husking)* You shouldn't a told her that.

DODGE: *(staring at T.V.)* What?

TILDEN: What you told her. You know.

DODGE: What do you know about it?

TILDEN: I know. I know all about it. We all know.

DODGE: So what difference does it make? Everybody knows, everybody's forgot.

TILDEN: She hasn't forgot.

DODGE: She should've forgot.

TILDEN: It's different for a woman. She couldn't forget that. How could she forget that?

DODGE: I don't want to talk about it!

TILDEN: What do you want to talk about?

DODGE: I don't want to talk about anything! I don't want to talk about troubles or what happened fifty years ago or thirty years ago or the race track or Florida or the last time I seeded the corn! I don't want to talk!

TILDEN: You don't wanna die do you?

DODGE: No, I don't wanna die either.

TILDEN: Well, you gotta talk or you'll die.

DODGE: Who told you that?

TILDEN: That's what I know. I found that out in New Mexico. I thought I was dying but I just lost my voice.

DODGE: Were you with somebody?

TILDEN: I was alone. I thought I was dead.

DODGE: Might as well have been. What'd you come back here for?

TILDEN: I didn't know where to go.

DODGE: You're a grown man. You shouldn't be needing your parents at your age. It's un-natural. There's nothing we can do for you now anyway. Couldn't you make a living down there? Couldn't you find some way to make a living? Support yourself? What'd'ya come back here for? You expect us to feed you forever?

TILDEN: I didn't know where else to go.

DODGE: I never went back to my parents. Never. Never even had the urge. I was independent. Always independent. Always found a way.

TILDEN: I didn't know what to do. I couldn't figure anything out.

DODGE: There's nothing to figure out. You just forge ahead. What's there to figure out?

TILDEN *stands.*

TILDEN: I don't know.

DODGE: Where are you going?

TILDEN: Out back.

DODGE: You're not supposed to go out there. You heard what she said. Don't play deaf with me!

TILDEN: I like it out there.

DODGE: In the rain?

TILDEN: Especially in the rain. I like the feeling of it. Feels like it always did.

DODGE: You're supposed to watch out for me. Get me things when I need them.

TILDEN: What do you need?

DODGE: I don't need anything! But I might. I might need something any second. Any second now. I can't be left alone for a minute!

DODGE *starts to cough.*

TILDEN: I'll be right outside. You can just yell.

DODGE: *(between coughs)* No! It's too far! You can't go out there! It's too far! You might not ever hear me!

TILDEN: *(moving to pills)* Why don't you take a pill? You want a pill?

DODGE *coughs more violently, throws himself back against sofa, clutches his throat.* TILDEN *stands by helplessly.*

DODGE: Water! Get me some water!

TILDEN *rushes off left.* DODGE *reaches out for the pills, knocking some bottles to the floor, coughing in spasms. He grabs a small bottle, takes out pills and swallows them.* TILDEN *rushes back on with a glass of water.* DODGE *takes it and drinks, his coughing subsides.*

TILDEN: You all right now?

DODGE *nods. Drinks more water.* TILDEN *moves in closer to him.* DODGE *sets glass of water on the night table. His coughing is almost gone.*

TILDEN: Why don't you lay down for a while? Just rest a little.

TILDEN *helps* DODGE *lay down on the sofa. Covers him with blanket.*

DODGE: You're not going outside are you?

TILDEN: No.

DODGE: I don't want to wake up and find you not here.

TILDEN: I'll be here.

TILDEN *tucks blanket around* DODGE.

DODGE: You'll stay right here?

TILDEN: I'll stay in my chair.

DODGE: That's not a chair. That's my old milking stool.

TILDEN: I know.

DODGE: Don't call it a chair.

TILDEN: I won't.

TILDEN *tries to take* DODGE'S *baseball cap off.*

DODGE: What're you doing! Leave that on me! Don't take that offa me! That's my cap!

TILDEN *leaves the cap on* DODGE.

TILDEN: I know.

DODGE: Bradley'll shave my head if I don't have that on. That's my cap.

TILDEN: I know it is.

DODGE: Don't take my cap off.

TILDEN: I won't.

DODGE: You stay right here now.

TILDEN: *(sits on stool)* I will.

DODGE: Don't go outside. There's nothing out there.

TILDEN: I won't.

DODGE: Everything's in here. Everything you need. Money's on the table. T.V. Is the T.V. on?

TILDEN: Yeah.

DODGE: Turn it off! Turn the damn thing off! What's it doing on?

TILDEN: *(shuts off t.v., light goes out)* You left it on.

DODGE: Well turn it off.

TILDEN: *(sits on stool again)* It's off.

DODGE: Leave it off.

TILDEN: I will.

DODGE: When I fall asleep you can turn it on.

TILDEN: Okay.

DODGE: You can watch the ball game. Red Sox. You like the Red Sox don't you?

TILDEN: Yeah.

DODGE: You can watch the Red Sox. Pee Wee Reese. Pee Wee Reese. You remember Pee Wee Reese?

TILDEN: No.

DODGE: Was he with the Red Sox?

TILDEN: I don't know.

DODGE: Pee Wee Reese. *(falling asleep)* You can watch the Cardinals. You remember Stan Musial.

TILDEN: No.

DODGE: Stan Musial. *(falling into sleep)* Bases loaded. Top a' the sixth. Bases loaded. Runner on first and third. Big fat knuckle ball. Floater. Big as a blimp. Cracko! Ball just took off like a rocket. Just pulverized. I marked it. Marked it with my eyes. Straight between the clock and the Burma Shave ad. I was the first kid out there. First kid. I had to fight hard for that ball. I wouldn't give it up. They almost tore the ears right off me. But I wouldn't give it up.

DODGE *falls into deep sleep.* TILDEN *just sits staring at him for a while. Slowly he leans toward the sofa, checking to see if* DODGE *is well asleep. He reaches slowly under the cushion and pulls out the bottle of booze.* DODGE *sleeps soundly.* TILDEN *stands quietly, staring at* DODGE *as he uncaps the bottle and takes a long drink. He caps the bottle and sticks it in his hip pocket. He looks around at the husks on the floor and then back to* DODGE. *He moves center stage and gathers an armload of corn husks then crosses back to the sofa. He stands holding the husks over* DODGE *and looking down at him he gently spreads the corn husks over the whole length of* DODGE'S *body. He stands back and looks at* DODGE. *Pulls out bottle, takes another drink, returns bottle to his hip pocket. He gathers more husks and repeats the procedure until the floor is clean of corn husks and* DODGE *is completely covered in them except for his head.* TILDEN *takes another long drink, stares at* DODGE *sleeping then quietly exits stage left. Long pause as the sound of rain continues.* DODGE *sleeps on. The figure of* BRADLEY *appears up left, outside the screen porch door. He holds a wet newspaper over his head as a protection from the rain. He seems to be struggling with the door then slips and almost falls to the ground.* DODGE *sleeps on, undisturbed.*

BRADLEY: Sonuvabitch! Sonuvagoddamnbitch!

BRADLEY *recovers his footing and makes it through the screen door onto the porch. He throws the newspaper down, shakes the water out of his hair, and brushes the rain off of his shoulders. He is a big man dressed in a grey sweat shirt, black suspenders, baggy dark blue pants and black janitor's shoes. His left leg is wooden, having been amputated above the knee. He moves with an exaggerated, almost mechanical limp. The squeaking sounds of leather and metal accompany his walk coming from the harness and hinges of the false leg. His arms and shoulders are extremely powerful and muscular due to a lifetime dependency on the upper torso doing all the work for the legs. He is about five years younger than* TILDEN. *He moves laboriously to the stage right door and enters, closing the door behind him. He doesn't notice* DODGE *at first. He moves toward the staircase.*

BRADLEY: *(calling to upstairs)* Mom!

He stops and listens. Turns upstage and sees DODGE *sleeping. Notices corn husks. He moves slowly toward sofa. Stops next to pail and looks into it. Looks at husks.* DODGE *stays asleep. Talks to himself.*

BRADLEY: What in the hell is this?

He looks at DODGE'S *sleeping face and shakes his head in disgust. He pulls out a pair of black electric hair clippers from his pocket. Unwinds the cord and crosses to the lamp. He jabs his wooden leg behind the knee, causing it to bend at the joint and awkwardly kneels to plug the cord into a floor outlet. He pulls himself to his feet again by using the sofa as leverage. He moves to* DODGE'S *head and again jabs his false leg. Goes down on one knee. He violently knocks away some of the corn husks then jerks off* DODGE'S *baseball cap and throws it down center stage.* DODGE *stays asleep.* BRADLEY *switches on the clippers. Lights start dimming.* BRADLEY *cuts* DODGE'S *hair while he sleeps. Lights dim slowly to black with the sound of clippers and rain.*

ACT 2

SCENE:

Same set as act 1. Night. Sound of rain. DODGE *still asleep on sofa. His hair is cut extremely short and in places the scalp is cut and bleeding. His cap is still center stage. All the corn and husks, pail and milking stool have been cleared away. The lights come up to the sound of a young girl laughing off stage left.* DODGE *remains asleep.* SHELLY *and* VINCE *appear up left outside the screen porch door sharing the shelter of* VINCE'S *overcoat above their heads.* SHELLY *is about nineteen, black hair, very beautiful. She wears tight jeans, high heels, purple T-shirt and a short rabbit fur coat. Her makeup is exaggerated and her hair has been curled.* VINCE *is* TILDEN'S *son, about twenty-two, wears a plaid shirt, jeans, dark glasses, cowboy boots and carries a black saxophone case. They shake the rain off themselves as they enter the porch through the screen door.*

SHELLY: *(laughing, gesturing to house)* This is it? I don't believe this is it!

VINCE: This is it.

SHELLY: This is the house?

VINCE: This is the house.

SHELLY: I don't believe it!

VINCE: How come?

SHELLY: It's like a Norman Rockwell cover or something.

VINCE: What's a' matter with that? It's American.

SHELLY: Where's the milkman and the little dog? What's the little dog's name? Spot. Spot and Jane. Dick and Jane and Spot.

VINCE: Knock it off.

SHELLY: Dick and Jane and Spot and Mom and Dad and Junior and Sissy!

She laughs. Slaps her knee.

VINCE: Come on! It's my heritage. What dya' expect?

She laughs more hysterically, out of control.

SHELLY: "And Tuffy and Toto and Dooda and Bonzo all went down one day to the corner grocery store to buy a big bag of licorice for Mr. Marshall's pussy cat!"

She laughs so hard she falls to her knees holding her stomach. VINCE *stands there looking at her.*

VINCE: Shelly will you get up!

She keeps laughing. Staggers to her feet. Turning in circles holding her stomach.

SHELLY: *(continuing her story in kid's voice)* "Mr. Marshall was on vacation. He had no idea that the four little boys had taken such a liking to his little kitty cat."

VINCE: Have some respect would ya'!

SHELLY: *(trying to control herself)* I'm sorry.

VINCE: Pull yourself together.

SHELLY: *(salutes him)* Yes sir.

She giggles.

VINCE: Jesus Christ, Shelly.

SHELLY: *(pause, smiling)* And Mr. Marshall—

VINCE: Cut it out.

She stops. Stands there staring at him. Stifles a giggle.

VINCE: *(after pause)* Are you finished?

SHELLY: Oh brother!

VINCE: I don't wanna go in there with you acting like an idiot.

SHELLY: Thanks.

VINCE: Well, I don't.

SHELLY: I won't embarrass you. Don't worry.

VINCE: I'm not worried.

SHELLY: You are too.

VINCE: Shelly look, I just don't wanna go in there with you giggling your head off. They might think something's wrong with you.

SHELLY: There is.

VINCE: There is not!

SHELLY: Something's definitely wrong with me.

VINCE: There is not!

SHELLY: There's something wrong with you too.

VINCE: There's nothing wrong with me either!

SHELLY: You wanna know what's wrong with you?

VINCE: What?

SHELLY *laughs.*

VINCE: *(crosses back left toward screen door)* I'm leaving!

SHELLY: *(stops laughing)* Wait! Stop. Stop! *(*VINCE *stops)* What's wrong with you is that you take the situation too seriously.

VINCE: I just don't want to have them think that I've suddenly arrived out of the middle of nowhere completely deranged.

SHELLY: What do you want them to think then?

VINCE: *(pause)* Nothing. Let's go in.

He crosses porch toward stage right interior door. SHELLY *follows him. The stage right door opens slowly.* VINCE *sticks his head in, doesn't notice* DODGE *sleeping. Calls out toward staircase.*

VINCE: Grandma!

SHELLY *breaks into laughter, unseen behind* VINCE. VINCE *pulls his head back outside and pulls door shut. We hear their voices again without seeing them.*

SHELLY'S VOICE: *(stops laughing)* I'm sorry. I'm sorry Vince. I really am. I really am sorry. I won't do it again. I couldn't help it.

VINCE'S VOICE: It's not all that funny.

SHELLY'S VOICE: I know it's not. I'm sorry.

VINCE'S VOICE: I mean this is a tense situation for me! I haven't seen them for over six years. I don't know what to expect.

SHELLY'S VOICE: I know. I won't do it again.

VINCE'S VOICE: Can't you bite your tongue or something?

SHELLY'S VOICE: Just don't say "Grandma," okay? *(she giggles, stops)* I mean if you say "Grandma" I don't know if I can stop myself.

VINCE'S VOICE: Well try!

SHELLY'S VOICE: Okay. Sorry.

Door opens again. VINCE *sticks his head in then enters.* SHELLY *follows behind him.* VINCE *crosses to staircase, sets down saxophone case and overcoat, looks up staircase.* SHELLY *notices* DODGE'S *baseball cap. Crosses to it. Picks it up and puts it on her head.* VINCE *goes up the stairs and disappears at the top.* SHELLY *watches him then turns and sees* DODGE *on the sofa. She takes off the baseball cap.*

VINCE'S VOICE: *(from above stairs)* Grandma!

SHELLY *crosses over to* DODGE *slowly and stands next to him. She stands at his head, reaches out slowly and touches one of the cuts. The second she touches his head,* DODGE *jerks up to a sitting position on the sofa, eyes open.* SHELLY *gasps.* DODGE *looks at her, sees his cap in her hands, quickly puts his hand to his bare head. He glares at* SHELLY *then whips the cap out of her hands and puts it on.* SHELLY *backs away from him.* DODGE *stares at her.*

SHELLY: I'm uh- with Vince.

DODGE *just glares at her.*

SHELLY: He's upstairs.

DODGE *looks at the staircase then back to* SHELLY.

SHELLY: *(calling upstairs)* Vince!

VINCE'S VOICE: Just a second!

SHELLY: You better get down here!

VINCE'S VOICE: Just a minute! I'm looking at the pictures.

DODGE *keeps staring at her.*

SHELLY: *(to* DODGE*)* We just got here. Pouring rain on the freeway so we thought we'd stop by. I mean Vince was planning on stopping anyway. He wanted to see you. He said he hadn't seen you in a long time.

Pause. DODGE *just keeps staring at her.*

SHELLY: We were going all the way through to New Mexico. To see his father. I guess his father lives out there. We thought we'd stop by and see you on the way. Kill two birds with one stone, you know? *(she laughs,* DODGE *stares, she stops laughing)* I mean Vince has this thing about his family now. I guess it's a new thing with him. I kind of find it hard to relate to. But he feels it's important. You know. I mean he feels he wants to get to know you all again. After all this time.

Pause. DODGE *just stares at her. She moves nervously to staircase and yells up to* VINCE.

SHELLY: Vince will you come down here please!

VINCE *comes half way down the stairs.*

VINCE: I guess they went out for a while.

SHELLY *points to sofa and* DODGE. VINCE *turns and sees* DODGE. *He comes all the way down staircase and crosses to* DODGE. SHELLY *stays behind near staircase, keeping her distance.*

VINCE: Grandpa?

DODGE *looks up at him, not recognizing him.*

DODGE: Did you bring the whiskey?

VINCE *looks back at* SHELLY *then back to* DODGE.

VINCE: Grandpa, it's Vince. I'm Vince. Tilden's son. You remember?

DODGE *stares at him.*

DODGE: You didn't do what you told me. You didn't stay here with me.

VINCE: Grandpa, I haven't been here until just now. I just got here.

DODGE: You left. You went outside like we told you not to do. You went out there in back. In the rain.

VINCE *looks back at* SHELLY. *She moves slowly toward sofa.*

SHELLY: Is he okay?

VINCE: I don't know. *(takes off his shades)* Look, Grandpa, don't you remember me? Vince. Your Grandson.

DODGE *stares at him then takes off his baseball cap.*

DODGE: *(points to his head)* See what happens when you leave me alone? See that? That's what happens.

VINCE *looks at his head.* VINCE *reaches out to touch his head.* DODGE *slaps his hand away with the cap and puts it back on his head.*

VINCE: What's going on Grandpa? Where's Halie?

DODGE: Don't worry about her. She won't be back for days. She says she'll be back but she won't be. *(he starts laughing)* There's life in the old girl yet! *(stops laughing)*

VINCE: How did you do that to your head?

DODGE: I didn't do it! Don't be ridiculous!

VINCE: Well who did then?

Pause. DODGE *stares at* VINCE.

DODGE: Who do you think did it? Who do you think?

SHELLY *moves toward* VINCE.

SHELLY: Vince, maybe we oughta' go. I don't like this. I mean this isn't my idea of a good time.

VINCE: *(to* SHELLY*)* Just a second. *(to* DODGE*)* Grandpa, look, I just got here. I just now got here. I haven't been here for six years. I don't know anything that's happened.

Pause. DODGE *stares at him.*

DODGE: You don't know anything?

VINCE: No.

DODGE: Well that's good. That's good. It's much better not to know anything. Much, much better.

VINCE: Isn't there anybody here with you?

DODGE *turns slowly and looks off to stage left.*

DODGE: Tilden's here.

VINCE: No, Grandpa, Tilden's in New Mexico. That's where I was going. I'm going out there to see him.

DODGE *turns slowly back to* VINCE.

DODGE: Tilden's here.

VINCE *backs away and joins* SHELLY. DODGE *stares at them.*

SHELLY: Vince, why don't we spend the night in a motel and come back in the morning? We could have breakfast. Maybe everything would be different.

VINCE: Don't be scared. There's nothing to be scared of. He's just old.

SHELLY: I'm not scared!

DODGE: You two are not my idea of the perfect couple!

SHELLY: *(after pause)* Oh really? Why's that?

VINCE: Shh! Don't aggravate him.

DODGE: There's something wrong between the two of you. Something not compatible.

VINCE: Grandpa, where did Halie go? Maybe we should call her.

DODGE: What are you talking about? Do you know what you're talking about? Are you just talking for the sake of talking? Lubricating the gums?

VINCE: I'm trying to figure out what's going on here!

DODGE: Is that it?

VINCE: Yes. I mean I expected everything to be different.

DODGE: Who are you to expect anything? Who are you supposed to be?

VINCE: I'm Vince! Your Grandson!

DODGE: Vince. My Grandson.

VINCE: Tilden's son.

DODGE: Tilden's son, Vince.

VINCE: You haven't seen me for a long time.

DODGE: When was the last time?

VINCE: I don't remember.

DODGE: You don't remember?

VINCE: No.

DODGE: You don't remember. How am I supposed to remember if you don't remember?

SHELLY: Vince, come on. This isn't going to work out.

VINCE: *(to* SHELLY*)* Just take it easy.

SHELLY: I'm taking it easy! He doesn't even know who you are!

VINCE: *(crossing toward* DODGE*)* Grandpa, Look—

DODGE: Stay where you are! Keep your distance!

VINCE *stops. Looks back at* SHELLY *then to* DODGE.

SHELLY: Vince, this is really making me nervous. I mean he doesn't even want us here. He doesn't even like us.

DODGE: She's a beautiful girl.

VINCE: Thanks.

DODGE: Very Beautiful Girl.

SHELLY: Oh my God.

DODGE: *(to* SHELLY*)* What's your name?

SHELLY: Shelly.

DODGE: Shelly. That's a man's name isn't it?

SHELLY: Not in this case.

DODGE: *(to* VINCE*)* She's a smart-ass too.

SHELLY: Vince! Can we go?

DODGE: She wants to go. She just got here and she wants to go.

VINCE: This is kind of strange for her.

DODGE: She'll get used to it. *(to* SHELLY*)* What part of the country do you come from?

SHELLY: Originally?

DODGE: That's right. Originally. At the very start.

SHELLY: L.A.

DODGE: L.A. Stupid country.

SHELLY: I can't stand this Vince! This is really unbelievable!

DODGE: It's stupid! L.A. is stupid! So is Florida! All those Sunshine States. They're all stupid! Do you know why they're stupid?

SHELLY: Illuminate me.

DODGE: I'll tell you why. Because they're full of smart-asses! That's why.

SHELLY *turns her back to* DODGE, *crosses to staircase and sits on bottom step.*

DODGE: *(to* VINCE*)* Now she's insulted.

VINCE: Well you weren't very polite.

DODGE: She's insulted! Look at her! In my house she's insulted! She's over there sulking because I insulted her!

SHELLY: *(to* VINCE*)* This is really terrific. This is wonderful. And you were worried about me making the right first impression!

DODGE: *(to* VINCE*)* She's a fireball isn't she? Regular fireball. I had some a' them in my day. Temporary stuff. Never lasted more than a week.

VINCE: Grandpa—

DODGE: Stop calling me Grandpa will ya'! It's sickening. "Grandpa." I'm nobody's Grandpa!

DODGE *starts feeling around under the cushion for the bottle of whiskey.* SHELLY *gets up from the staircase.*

SHELLY: *(to* VINCE*)* Maybe you've got the wrong house. Did you ever think of that? Maybe this is the wrong address!

VINCE: It's not the wrong address! I recognize the yard.

SHELLY: Yeah but do you recognize the people? He says he's not your Grandfather.

DODGE: *(digging for bottle)* Where's that bottle!

VINCE: He's just sick or something. I don't know what's happened to him.

DODGE: Where's my goddamn bottle!

DODGE *gets up from sofa and starts tearing the cushions off it and throwing them downstage, looking for the whiskey.*

SHELLY: Can't we just drive on to New Mexico? This is terrible, Vince! I don't want to stay here. In this house. I thought it was going to be turkey dinners and apple pie and all that kinda stuff.

VINCE: Well I hate to disappoint you!

SHELLY: I'm not disappointed! I'm fuckin' terrified! I wanna' go!

DODGE *yells toward stage left.*

DODGE: Tilden! Tilden!

DODGE *keeps ripping away at the sofa looking for his bottle, he knocks over the night stand with the bottles.* VINCE *and* SHELLY *watch as he starts ripping the stuffing out of the sofa.*

VINCE: *(to* SHELLY*)* He's lost his mind or something. I've got to try to help him.

SHELLY: You help him! I'm leaving!

SHELLY *starts to leave.* VINCE *grabs her. They struggle as* DODGE *keeps ripping away at the sofa and yelling.*

DODGE: Tilden! Tilden get your ass in here! Tilden!

SHELLY: Let go of me!

VINCE: You're not going anywhere! You're going to stay right here!

SHELLY: Let go of me you sonuvabitch! I'm not your property!

Suddenly TILDEN *walks on from stage left just as he did before. This time his arms are full of carrots.* DODGE, VINCE *and* SHELLY *stop suddenly when they see him. They all stare at* TILDEN *as he crosses slowly center stage with the carrots and stops.* DODGE *sits on sofa, exhausted.*

DODGE: *(panting, to* TILDEN*)* Where in the hell have you been?

TILDEN: Out back.

DODGE: Where's my bottle?

TILDEN: Gone.

TILDEN *and* VINCE *stare at each other.* SHELLY *backs away.*

DODGE: *(to* TILDEN*)* You stole my bottle!

VINCE: *(to* TILDEN*)* Dad?

TILDEN *just stares at* VINCE.

DODGE: You had no right to steal my bottle! No right at all!

VINCE: *(to* TILDEN*)* It's Vince. I'm Vince.

TILDEN *stares at* VINCE *then looks at* DODGE *then turns to* SHELLY.

TILDEN: *(after pause)* I picked these carrots. If anybody wants any carrots, I picked 'em.

SHELLY: *(to* VINCE*)* This is your father?

VINCE: *(to* TILDEN*)* Dad, what're you doing here?

TILDEN *just stares at* VINCE, *holding carrots,* DODGE *pulls the blanket back over himself.*

DODGE: *(to* TILDEN*)* You're going to have to get me another bottle! You gotta get me a bottle before Halie comes back! There's money on the table. *(points to stage left kitchen)*

TILDEN: *(shaking his head)* I'm not going down there. Into town.

SHELLY *crosses to* TILDEN. TILDEN *stares at her.*

SHELLY: *(to* TILDEN*)* Are you Vince's father?

TILDEN: *(to* SHELLY*)* Vince?

SHELLY: *(pointing to* VINCE*)* This is supposed to be your son! Is he your son? Do you recognize him? I'm just along for the ride here. I thought everybody knew each other!

TILDEN *stares at* VINCE. DODGE *wraps himself up in the blanket and sits on sofa staring at the floor.*

TILDEN: I had a son once but we buried him.

DODGE *quickly looks at* TILDEN. SHELLY *looks to* VINCE.

DODGE: You shut up about that! You don't know anything about that!

VINCE: Dad, I thought you were in New Mexico. We were going to drive down there and see you.

TILDEN: Long way to drive.

DODGE: *(to* TILDEN*)* You don't know anything about that! That happened before you were born! Long before!

VINCE: What's happened, Dad? What's going on here? I thought everything was all right. What's happened to Halie?

TILDEN: She left.

SHELLY: *(to* TILDEN*)* Do you want me to take those carrots for you?
TILDEN stares at her. She moves in close to him. Holds out her arms. TILDEN stares at her arms then slowly dumps the carrots into her arms. SHELLY stands there holding the carrots.

TILDEN: *(to* SHELLY*)* You like Carrots?

SHELLY: Sure. I like all kinds of vegetables.

DODGE: *(to* TILDEN*)* You gotta get me a bottle before Halie comes back!
DODGE hits sofa with his fist. VINCE *crosses up to* DODGE *and tries to console him.* SHELLY *and* TILDEN *stay facing each other.*

TILDEN: *(to* SHELLY*)* Back yard's full of carrots. Corn. Potatoes.

SHELLY: You're Vince's father, right?

TILDEN: All kinds of vegetables. You like vegetables?

SHELLY: *(laughs)* Yeah. I love vegetables.

TILDEN: We could cook these carrots ya' know. You could cut 'em up and we could cook 'em.

SHELLY: All right.

TILDEN: I'll get you a pail and a knife.

SHELLY: Okay.

TILDEN: I'll be right back. Don't go.
TILDEN exits off stage left. SHELLY *stands center, arms full of carrots.* VINCE *stands next to* DODGE. SHELLY *looks toward* VINCE *then down at the carrots.*

DODGE: *(to* VINCE*)* You could get me a bottle. *(pointing off left)* There's money on the table.

VINCE: Grandpa why don't you lay down for a while?

DODGE: I don't wanna lay down for a while! Every time I lay down something happens! *(whips off his cap, points at his head)* Look what happens! That's what happens! *(pulls his cap back on)* You go lie down and see what happens to you! See how you like it! They'll steal your bottle! They'll cut your hair! They'll murder your children! That's what'll happen.

VINCE: Just relax for a while.

DODGE: *(pause)* You could get me a bottle ya' know. There's nothing stopping you from getting me a bottle.

SHELLY: Why don't you get him a bottle Vince? Maybe it would help everybody identify each other.

DODGE: *(pointing to* SHELLY*)* There, see? She thinks you should get me a bottle.

VINCE *crosses to* SHELLY.

VINCE: What're you doing with those carrots.

SHELLY: I'm waiting for your father.

DODGE: She thinks you should get me a bottle!

VINCE: Shelly put the carrots down will ya'! We gotta deal with the situation here! I'm gonna need your help.

SHELLY: I'm helping.

VINCE: You're only adding to the problem! You're making things worse! Put the carrots down!

VINCE *tries to knock the carrots out of her arms. She turns away from him, protecting the carrots.*

SHELLY: Get away from me! Stop it!

VINCE *stands back from her. She turns to him still holding the carrots.*

VINCE: *(to* SHELLY*)* Why are you doing this! Are you trying to make fun of me? This is my family you know!

SHELLY: You coulda' fooled me! I'd just as soon not be here myself. I'd just as soon be a thousand miles from here. I'd rather be anywhere but here. You're the one who wants to stay. So I'll stay. I'll stay and I'll cut the carrots. And I'll cook the carrots. And I'll do whatever I have to do to survive. Just to make it through this.

VINCE: Put the carrots down Shelly.

TILDEN *enters from left with pail, milking stool and a knife. He sets the stool and pail center stage for* SHELLY. SHELLY *looks at* VINCE *then sits down on stool, sets the carrots on the floor and takes the knife from* TILDEN. *She looks at* VINCE *again then picks up a carrot, cuts the ends off, scrapes it and drops it in pail. She repeats this,* VINCE *glares at her. She smiles.*

DODGE: She could get me a bottle. She's the type a' girl that could get me a bottle. Easy. She'd go down there. Slink up to the counter. They'd probably give her two bottles for the price of one. She could do that.

SHELLY *laughs. Keeps cutting carrots.* VINCE *crosses up to* DODGE, *looks at him.* TILDEN *watches* SHELLY'S *hands. Long pause.*

VINCE: *(to* DODGE*)* I haven't changed that much. I mean physically. Physically I'm just about the same. Same size. Same weight. Everything's the same.

DODGE *keeps staring at* SHELLY *while* VINCE *talks to him.*

DODGE: She's a beautiful girl. Exceptional.

VINCE *moves in front of* DODGE *to block his view of* SHELLY. DODGE *keeps craning his head around to see her as* VINCE *demonstrates tricks from his past.*

VINCE: Look. Look at this. Do you remember this? I used to bend my thumb behind my knuckles. You remember? I used to do it at the dinner table.

VINCE *bends a thumb behind his knuckles for* DODGE *and holds it out to him.* DODGE *takes a short glance then looks back at* SHELLY. VINCE *shifts position and shows him something else.*

VINCE: What about this?

VINCE *curls his lips back and starts drumming on his teeth with his fingernails making little tapping sounds.* DODGE *watches a while.* TILDEN *turns toward the sound.* VINCE *keeps it up. He sees* TILDEN *taking notice and crosses to* TILDEN *as he drums on his teeth.* DODGE *turns T.V. on. watches it.*

VINCE: You remember this Dad?

VINCE *keeps on drumming for* TILDEN. TILDEN *watches a while, fascinated, then turns back to* SHELLY. VINCE *keeps up the drumming on his teeth, crosses back to* DODGE *doing it.* SHELLY *keeps working on carrots, talking to* TILDEN.

SHELLY: *(to* TILDEN*)* He drives me crazy with that sometimes.

VINCE: *(to* DODGE*)* I Know! Here's one you'll remember. You used to kick me out of the house for this one.

VINCE *pulls his shirt out of his belt and holds it tucked under his chin with his stomach exposed. He grabs the flesh on either side of his belly button and pushes it in and out to make it look like a mouth talking. He watches his belly button and makes a deep sounding cartoon voice to synchronize with the movement. He demonstrates it to* DODGE *then crosses down to* TILDEN *doing it. Both* DODGE *and* TILDEN *take short, uninterested glances then ignore him.*

VINCE: *(deep cartoon voice)* "Hello. How are you? I'm fine. Thank you very much. It's so good to see you looking well this fine Sunday morning. I was going down to the hardware store to fetch a pail of water."

SHELLY: Vince, don't be pathetic will ya'!

VINCE *stops. Tucks his shirt back in.*

SHELLY: Jesus Christ. They're not gonna play. Can't you see that?

SHELLY *keeps cutting carrots.* VINCE *slowly moves toward* TILDEN. TILDEN *keeps watching* SHELLY. DODGE *watches T.V.*

VINCE: *(to* SHELLY*)* I don't get it. I really don't get it. Maybe it's me. Maybe I forgot something.

DODGE: *(from sofa)* You forgot to get me a bottle! That's what you forgot. Anybody in this house could get me a bottle. Anybody! But nobody will. Nobody understands the urgency! Peelin carrots is more important. Playin piano on your teeth! Well I hope you all remember this when you get up in years. When you find yourself immobilized. Dependent on the whims of others.

VINCE *moves up toward* DODGE. *Pause as he looks at him.*

VINCE: I'll get you a bottle.

DODGE: You will?

VINCE: Sure.

SHELLY *stands holding knife and carrot.*

SHELLY: You're not going to leave me here are you?

VINCE: *(moving to her)* You suggested it! You said, "why don't I go get him a bottle." So I'll go get him a bottle!

SHELLY: But I can't stay here.

VINCE: What is going on! A minute ago you were ready to cut carrots all night!

SHELLY: That was only if you stayed. Something to keep me busy, so I wouldn't be so nervous. I don't want to stay here alone.

DODGE: Don't let her talk you out of it! She's a bad influence. I could see it the minute she stepped in here.

SHELLY: *(to* DODGE*)* You were asleep!

TILDEN: *(to* SHELLY*)* Don't you want to cut carrots anymore?

SHELLY: Sure. Sure I do.

SHELLY *sits back down on stool and continues cutting carrots. Pause.* VINCE *moves around, stroking his hair, staring at* DODGE *and* TILDEN. VINCE *and* SHELLY *exchange glances.* DODGE *watches T.V.*

VINCE: Boy! This is amazing. This is truly amazing. *(keeps moving around)* What is this anyway? Am I in a time warp or something? Have I committed an unpardonable offence? It's true, I'm not married. (SHELLY *looks at him, then back to carrots*) But I'm also not divorced. I have been known to plunge into sinful infatuation with the Alto Saxophone. Sucking on number 5 reeds deep into the wee wee hours.

SHELLY: Vince, what are you doing that for? They don't care about any of that. They just don't recognize you, that's all.

VINCE: How could they not recognize me! How in the hell could they not recognize me! I'm their son!

DODGE: *(watching t.v.)* You're no son of mine. I've had sons in my time and you're not one of 'em.

Long pause. VINCE *stares at* DODGE *then looks at* TILDEN. *He turns to* SHELLY.

VINCE: Shelly, I gotta go out for a while. I just gotta go out. I'll get a bottle and I'll come right back. You'll be o.k. here. Really.

SHELLY: I don't know if I can handle this Vince.

VINCE: I just gotta think or something. I don't know. I gotta put this all together.

SHELLY: Can't we just go?

VINCE: No! I gotta find out what's going on.

SHELLY: Look, you think you're bad off, what about me? Not only don't they recognize me but I've never seen them before in my life. I don't know who these guys are. They could be anybody!

VINCE: They're not anybody!

SHELLY: That's what you say.

VINCE: They're my family for Christ's sake! I should know who my own family is! Now give me a break. It won't take that long. I'll just go out and I'll come right back. Nothing'll happen. I promise.

SHELLY *stares at him. Pause.*

SHELLY: All right.

VINCE: Thanks. *(he crosses up to* DODGE*)* I'm gonna go out now, Grandpa and I'll pick you up a bottle. Okay?

DODGE: Change of heart huh? *(pointing off left)* Money's on the table. In the kitchen.

VINCE *moves toward* SHELLY.

VINCE: *(to* SHELLY*)* You be all right?

SHELLY: *(cutting carrots)* Sure. I'm fine. I'll just keep real busy while you're gone.

VINCE *looks at* TILDEN *who keeps staring down at* SHELLY'S *hands.*

DODGE: Persistence see? That's what it takes. Persistence. Persistence, fortitude and determination. Those are the three virtues. You stick with those three and you can't go wrong.

VINCE: *(to* TILDEN*)* You want anything, Dad?

TILDEN: *(looks up at* VINCE*)* Me?

VINCE: From the store? I'm gonna get grandpa a bottle.

TILDEN: He's not supposed to drink. Halie wouldn't like it.

VINCE: He wants a bottle.

TILDEN: He's not supposed to drink.

DODGE: *(to* VINCE*)* Don't negotiate with him! Don't make any transactions until you've spoken to me first! He'll steal you blind!

VINCE: *(to* DODGE*)* Tilden says you're not supposed to drink.

DODGE: Tilden's lost his marbles! Look at him! He's around the bend. Take a look at him.

VINCE stares at TILDEN. *TILDEN watches* SHELLY'S *hands as she keeps cutting carrots.*

DODGE: Now look at me. Look here at me!

VINCE looks back to DODGE.

DODGE: Now, between the two of us, who do you think is more trustworthy? Him or me? Can you trust a man who keeps bringing in vegetables from out of nowhere? Take a look at him.

VINCE looks back at TILDEN.

SHELLY: Go get the bottle Vince.

VINCE: *(to* SHELLY*)* You sure you'll be all right?

SHELLY: I'll be fine. I feel right at home now.

VINCE: You do?

SHELLY: I'm fine. Now that I've got the carrots everything is all right.

VINCE: I'll be right back.

VINCE crosses stage left.

DODGE: Where are you going?

VINCE: I'm going to get the money.

DODGE: Then where are you going?

VINCE: Liquor store.

DODGE: Don't go anyplace else. Don't go off some place and drink. Come right back here.

VINCE: I will.

VINCE exits stage left.

DODGE: *(calling after* VINCE*)* You've got responsibility now! And don't go out the back way either! Come out through this way! I wanna' see you when you leave! Don't go out the back!

VINCE'S VOICE: *(off left)* I won't!

DODGE *turns and looks at* TILDEN *and* SHELLY.

DODGE: Untrustworthy. Probably drown himself if he went out the back. Fall right in a hole. I'd never get my bottle.

SHELLY: I wouldn't worry about Vince. He can take care of himself.

DODGE: Oh he can, huh? Independent.

VINCE *comes on again from stage left with two dollars in his hand. He crosses stage right past* DODGE.

DODGE: *(to* VINCE*)* You got the money?

VINCE: Yeah. Two bucks.

DODGE: Two bucks. Two bucks is two bucks. Don't sneer.

VINCE: What kind do you want?

DODGE: Whiskey! Gold Star Sour Mash. Use your own discretion.

VINCE: Okay.

VINCE *crosses to stage right door. Opens it. Stops when he hears* TILDEN.

TILDEN: *(to* VINCE*)* You drove all the way from New Mexico?

VINCE *turns and looks at* TILDEN. *They stare at each other.* VINCE *shakes his head, goes out the door, crosses porch and exits out screen door.* TILDEN *watches him go. Pause.*

SHELLY: You really don't recognize him? Either one of you?

TILDEN *turns again and stares at* SHELLY'S *hands as she cuts carrots.*

DODGE: *(watching t.v.)* Recognize who?

SHELLY: Vince.

DODGE: What's to recognize?

DODGE *lights a cigarette, coughs slightly and stares at t.v.*

SHELLY: It'd be cruel if you recognized him and didn't tell him. Wouldn't be fair.

DODGE *just stares at t.v., smoking.*

TILDEN: I thought I recognized him. I thought I recognized something about him.

SHELLY: You did?

TILDEN: I thought I saw a face inside his face.

SHELLY: Well it was probably that you saw what he used to look like. You haven't seen him for six years.

TILDEN: I haven't?

SHELLY: That's what he says.

TILDEN *moves around in front of her as she continues with carrots.*

TILDEN: Where was it I saw him last?

SHELLY: I don't know. I've only known him for a few months. He doesn't tell me everything.

TILDEN: He doesn't?

SHELLY: Not stuff like that.

TILDEN: What does he tell you?

SHELLY: You mean in general?

TILDEN: Yeah.

TILDEN *moves around behind her.*

SHELLY: Well he tells me all kinds of things.

TILDEN: Like what?

SHELLY: I don't know! I mean I can't just come right out and tell you how he feels.

TILDEN: How come?

TILDEN *keeps moving around her slowly in a circle.*

SHELLY: Because it's stuff he told me privately!

TILDEN: And you can't tell me?

SHELLY: I don't even know you!

DODGE: Tilden, go out in the kitchen and make me some coffee! Leave the girl alone.

SHELLY: *(to* DODGE*)* He's all right.

TILDEN *ignores* DODGE, *keeps moving around* SHELLY. *He stares at her hair and coat.* DODGE *stares at t.v.*

TILDEN: You mean you can't tell me anything?

SHELLY: I can tell you some things. I mean we can have a conversation.

TILDEN: We can?

SHELLY: Sure. We're having a conversation right now.

TILDEN: We are?

SHELLY: Yes. That's what we're doing.

TILDEN: But there's certain things you can't tell me, right?

SHELLY: Right.

TILDEN: There's certain things I can't tell you either.

SHELLY: How come?

TILDEN: I don't know. Nobody's supposed to hear it.

SHELLY: Well, you can tell me anything you want to.

TILDEN: I can?

SHELLY: Sure.

TILDEN: It might not be very nice.

SHELLY: That's all right. I've been around.

TILDEN: It might be awful.

SHELLY: Well, can't you tell me anything nice?

TILDEN *stops in front of her and stares at her coat.* SHELLY *looks back at him. Long pause.*

TILDEN: *(after pause)* Can I touch your coat?

SHELLY: My coat? *(she looks at her coat then back to* TILDEN*)* Sure.

TILDEN: You don't mind?

SHELLY: No. Go ahead.

SHELLY *holds her arm out for* TILDEN *to touch.* DODGE *stays fixed on t.v.* TILDEN *moves in slowly toward* SHELLY, *staring at her arm. He reaches out very slowly and touches her arm, feels the fur gently then draws his hand back.* SHELLY *keeps her arm out.*

SHELLY: It's rabbit.

TILDEN: Rabbit.

He reaches out again very slowly and touches the fur on her arm then pulls back his hand again. SHELLY *drops her arm.*

SHELLY: My arm was getting tired.

TILDEN: Can I hold it?

SHELLY: *(pause)* The coat? Sure.

SHELLY *takes off her coat and hands it to* TILDEN. TILDEN *takes it slowly, feels the fur then puts it on.* SHELLY *watches as* TILDEN *strokes the fur slowly. He smiles at her. She goes back to cutting carrots.*

SHELLY: You can have it if you want.

TILDEN: I can?

SHELLY: Yeah. I've got a raincoat in the car. That's all I need.

TILDEN: You've got a car?

SHELLY: Vince does.

TILDEN *walks around stroking the fur and smiling at the coat.* SHELLY *watches him when he's not looking.* DODGE *sticks with t.v., stretches out on sofa wrapped in blanket.*

TILDEN: *(as he walks around)* I had a car once! I had a white car! I drove. I went everywhere. I went to the mountains. I drove in the snow.

SHELLY: That must've been fun.

TILDEN: *(still moving, feeling coat)* I drove all day long sometimes. Across the desert. Way out across the desert. I drove past towns. Anywhere. Past Palm trees. Lightening. Anything. I would drive through it. I would drive through it and I would stop and I would look around and I would drive on. I would get back in and drive!

I loved to drive. There was nothing I loved more. Nothing I dreamed of was better than driving.

DODGE: *(eyes on t.v.)* Pipe down would ya'!

TILDEN *stops. Stares at* SHELLY.

SHELLY: Do you do much driving now?

TILDEN: Now? Now? I don't drive now.

SHELLY: How come?

TILDEN: I'm grown up now.

SHELLY: Grown up?

TILDEN: I'm not a kid.

SHELLY: You don't have to be a kid to drive.

TILDEN: It wasn't driving then.

SHELLY: What was it?

TILDEN: Adventure. I went everywhere.

SHELLY: Well you can still do that.

TILDEN: Not now.

SHELLY: Why not?

TILDEN: I just told you. You don't understand anything. If I told you something you wouldn't understand it.

SHELLY: Told me what?

TILDEN: Told you something that's true.

SHELLY: Like what?

TILDEN: Like a baby. Like a little tiny baby.

SHELLY: Like when you were little?

TILDEN: If I told you you'd make me give your coat back.

SHELLY: I won't. I promise. Tell me.

TILDEN: I can't. Dodge won't let me.

SHELLY: He won't hear you. It's okay.

Pause. TILDEN *stares at her. Moves slightly toward her.*

TILDEN: We had a baby. *(motioning to* DODGE*)* He did. Dodge did. Could pick it up with one hand. Put it in the other. Little baby. Dodge killed it.

SHELLY *stands.*

TILDEN: Don't stand up. Don't stand up!

SHELLY *sits again.* DODGE *sits up on sofa and looks at them.*

TILDEN: Dodge drowned it.

SHELLY: Don't tell me anymore! Okay?

TILDEN *moves closer to her.* DODGE *takes more interest.*

DODGE: Tilden? You leave that girl alone!

TILDEN: *(pays no attention)* Never told Halie. Never told anybody. Just drowned it.

DODGE: *(shuts off t.v.)* Tilden!

TILDEN: Nobody could find it. Just disappeared. Cops looked for it. Neighbors. Nobody could find it.

DODGE *struggles to get up from sofa.*

DODGE: Tilden, what're you telling her! Tilden!

DODGE *keeps struggling until he's standing.*

TILDEN: Finally everybody just gave up. Just stopped looking. Everybody had a different answer. Kidnap. Murder. Accident. Some kind of accident.

DODGE *struggles to walk toward* TILDEN *and falls.* TILDEN *ignores him.*

DODGE: Tilden you shut up! You shut up about it!

DODGE *starts coughing on the floor.* SHELLY *watches him from the stool.*

TILDEN: Little tiny baby just disappeared. It's not hard. It's so small. Almost invisible.

SHELLY *makes a move to help* DODGE. TILDEN *firmly pushes her back down on the stool.* DODGE *keeps coughing.*

TILDEN: He said he had his reasons. Said it went a long way back. But he wouldn't tell anybody.

DODGE: Tilden! Don't tell her anything! Don't tell her!

TILDEN: He's the only one who knows where it's buried. The only one. Like a secret buried treasure. Won't tell any of us. Won't tell me or mother or even Bradley. Especially Bradley. Bradley tried to force it out of him but he wouldn't tell. Wouldn't even tell why he did it. One night he just did it.

DODGE'S *coughing subsides.* SHELLY *stays on stool staring at* DODGE. TILDEN *slowly takes* SHELLY'S *coat off and holds it out to her. Long pause.* SHELLY *sits there trembling.*

TILDEN: You probably want your coat back now.

SHELLY *stares at coat but doesn't move to take it. The sound of* BRADLEY'S *leg squeaking is heard off left. The others on stage remain still.* BRADLEY *appears up left outside the screen door wearing a yellow rain slicker. He enters through screen door, crosses porch to stage right door and enters stage. Closes door. Takes off rain slicker and shakes it out. He sees all the others and stops.* TILDEN *turns to him.* BRADLEY *stares at* SHELLY. DODGE *remains on floor.*

BRADLEY: What's going on here? *(motioning to* SHELLY*)* Who's that?

SHELLY *stands, moves back away from* BRADLEY *as he crosses toward her. He stops next to* TILDEN. *He sees coat in* TILDEN'S *hand and grabs it away from him.*

BRADLEY: Who's she supposed to be?

TILDEN: She's driving to New Mexico.

BRADLEY *stares at her.* SHELLY *is frozen.* BRADLEY *limps over to her with the coat in his fist. He stops in front of her.*

BRADLEY: *(to* SHELLY, *after pause)* Vacation?

SHELLY *shakes her head "no", trembling.*

BRADLEY: *(to* SHELLY, *motioning to* TILDEN*)* You taking him with you?

SHELLY *shakes her head "no".* BRADLEY *crosses back to* TILDEN.

BRADLEY: You oughta'. No use leaving him here. Doesn't do a lick a' work. Doesn't raise a finger. *(stopping, to* TILDEN*)* Do ya' *(to* SHELLY*)* 'Course he used to be an All American. Quarterback or Fullback or somethin'. He tell you that?

SHELLY *shakes her head "no".*

BRADLEY: Yeah, he used to be a big deal. Wore lettermen's sweaters. Had medals hanging all around his neck. Real purty. Big deal. *(he laughs to himself, notices* DODGE *on floor, crosses to him, stops)* This one too. *(to* SHELLY*)* You'd never think it to look at him would ya'? All bony and wasted away.

SHELLY *shakes her head again.* BRADLEY *stares at her, crosses back to her, clenching the coat in his fist. He stops in front of* SHELLY.

BRADLEY: Women like that kinda' thing don't they?

SHELLY: What?

BRADLEY: Importance. Importance in a man?

SHELLY: I don't know.

BRADLEY: Yeah. You know, you know. Don't give me that. *(moves closer to* SHELLY*)* You're with Tilden?

SHELLY: No.

BRADLEY: *(turning to* TILDEN*)* Tilden! She with you?

TILDEN *doesn't answer. Stares at floor.*

BRADLEY: Tilden!

TILDEN *suddenly bolts and runs off up stage left.* BRADLEY *laughs. Talks to* SHELLY. DODGE *starts moving his lips silently as though talking to someone invisible on the floor.*

BRADLEY: *(laughing)* Scared to death! He was always scared!

BRADLEY *stops laughing. Stares at* SHELLY.

BRADLEY: You're scared too, right? *(laughs again)* You're scared and you don't even know me. *(stops laughing)* You don't gotta be scared.

SHELLY *looks at* DODGE *on the floor.*

SHELLY: Can't we do something for him?

BRADLEY: *(looking at* DODGE*)* We could shoot him. *(laughs)* We could drown him! What about drowning him?

SHELLY: Shut up!

BRADLEY *stops laughing. Moves in closer to* SHELLY. *She freezes.* BRADLEY *speaks slowly and deliberately.*

BRADLEY: Hey! Missus. Don't talk to me like that. Don't talk to me in that tone a' voice. There was a time when I had to take that tone a' voice from pretty near everyone. *(motioning to* DODGE*)* Him, for one! Him and that half brain that just ran outa' here. They don't talk to me like that now. Not any more. Everything's turned around now. Full circle. Isn't that funny?

SHELLY: I'm sorry.

BRADLEY: Open your mouth.

SHELLY: What?

BRADLEY: *(motioning for her to open her mouth)* Open up.

She opens her mouth slightly.

BRADLEY: Wider.

She opens her mouth wider.

BRADLEY: Keep it like that.

She does. Stares at BRADLEY. *With his free hand he puts his fingers into her mouth. She tries to pull away.*

BRADLEY: Just stay put!

She freezes. He keeps his fingers in her mouth. Stares at her. Pause. He pulls his hand out. She closes her mouth, keeps her eyes on him. BRADLEY *smiles. He looks at* DODGE *on the floor and crosses over to him.* SHELLY *watches him closely.* BRADLEY *stands over* DODGE *and smiles at* SHELLY. *He holds her coat up in both hands over* DODGE, *keeps smiling at* SHELLY. *He looks down at* DODGE *then drops the coat so that it lands on* DODGE *and covers his head.* BRADLEY *keeps his hands up in the position of holding the coat, looks over at* SHELLY *and smiles. The lights black out.*

ACT 3

SCENE:

Same set. Morning. Bright sun. No sound of rain. Everything has been cleared up again. No sign of carrots. No pail. No stool. VINCE'S *saxophone case and overcoat are still at the foot of the staircase.* BRADLEY *is asleep on the sofa under* DODGE'S *blanket. His head toward stage left.* BRADLEY'S *wooden leg is leaning against the sofa right by his head. The shoe is left on it. The harness hangs down.* DODGE *is sitting on the floor, propped up against the t.v. set facing stage left wearing his baseball cap.* SHELLY'S *rabbit fur coat covers his chest and shoulders. He stares off toward stage left. He seems weaker and more disoriented. The lights rise slowly to the sound of birds and remain for a while in silence on the two men.* BRADLEY *sleeps very soundly.* DODGE *hardly moves.* SHELLY *appears from stage left with a big smile, slowly crossing toward* DODGE *balancing a steaming cup of broth in a saucer.* DODGE *just stares at her as she gets close to him.*

SHELLY: *(as she crosses)* This is going to make all the difference in the world, Grandpa. You don't mind me calling you Grandpa do you? I mean I know you minded when Vince called you that but you don't even know him.

DODGE: He skipped town with my money ya' know. I'm gonna hold you as collateral.

SHELLY: He'll be back. Don't you worry.

She kneels down next to DODGE *and puts the cup and saucer in his lap.*

DODGE: It's morning already! Not only didn't I get my bottle but he's got my two bucks!

SHELLY: Try to drink this, okay? Don't spill it.

DODGE: What is it?

SHELLY: Beef bouillon. It'll warm you up.

DODGE: Bouillon! I don't want any goddamn bouillon! Get that stuff away from me!

SHELLY: I just got through making it.

DODGE: I don't care if you just spent all week making it! I ain't drinking it!

SHELLY: Well, what am I supposed to do with it then? I'm trying to help you out. Besides, it's good for you.

DODGE: Get it away from me!

SHELLY *stands up with cup and saucer.*

DODGE: What do you know what's good for me anyway?

She looks at DODGE *then turns away from him, crossing to staircase, sits on bottom step and drinks the bouillon.* DODGE *stares at her.*

DODGE: You know what'd be good for me?

SHELLY: What?

DODGE: A little massage. A little contact.

SHELLY: Oh no. I've had enough contact for a while. Thanks anyway.

She keeps sipping bouillon, stays sitting. Pause as DODGE *stares at her.*

DODGE: Why not? You got nothing better to do. That fella's not gonna be back here. You're not expecting him to show up again are you?

SHELLY: Sure. He'll show up. He left his horn here.

DODGE: His horn? *(laughs)* You're his horn?

SHELLY: Very funny.

DODGE: He's run off with my money! He's not coming back here.

SHELLY: He'll be back.

DODGE: You're a funny chicken, you know that?

SHELLY: Thanks.

DODGE: Full of faith. Hope. Faith and hope. You're all alike you hopers. If it's not God then it's a man. If it's not a man then it's a woman. If its not a woman then its the land or the future of some kind. Some kind of future.

Pause.

SHELLY: *(looking toward porch)* I'm glad it stopped raining.

DODGE: *(looks toward porch then back to her)* That's what I mean. See, you're glad it stopped raining. Now you think everything's gonna be different. Just 'cause the sun comes out.

SHELLY: It's already different. Last night I was scared.

DODGE: Scared a' what?

SHELLY: Just scared.

DODGE: Bradley? *(looks at* BRADLEY*)* He's a push-over. 'Specially now. All ya' gotta' do is take his leg and throw it out the back door. Helpless. Totally helpless.

SHELLY *turns and stares at* BRADLEY'S *wooden leg then looks at* DODGE. *She sips bouillon.*

SHELLY: You'd do that?

DODGE: Me? I've hardly got the strength to breathe.

SHELLY: But you'd actually do it if you could?

DODGE: Don't be so easily shocked, girlie. There's nothing a man can't do. You dream it up and he can do it. Anything.

SHELLY: You've tried I guess.

DODGE: Don't sit there sippin' your bouillon and judging me! This is my house!

SHELLY: I forgot.

DODGE: You forgot? Whose house did you think it was?

SHELLY: Mine.

DODGE *just stares at her. Long pause. She sips from cup.*

SHELLY: I know it's not mine but I had that feeling.

DODGE: What feeling?

SHELLY: The feeling that nobody lives here but me. I mean everybody's gone. You're here, but it doesn't seem like you're supposed to be. *(pointing to* BRADLEY*)* Doesn't seem like he's supposed to be here either. I don't know what it is. It's the house or something. Something familiar. Like I know my way around here. Did you ever get that feeling?

DODGE *stares at her in silence. Pause.*

DODGE: No. No, I never did.

SHELLY *gets up. Moves around space holding cup.*

SHELLY: Last night I went to sleep up there in that room.

DODGE: What room?

SHELLY: That room up there with all the pictures. All the crosses on the wall.

DODGE: Halie's room?

SHELLY: Yeah. Whoever "Halie" is.

DODGE: She's my wife.

SHELLY: So you remember her?

DODGE: Whad'ya mean! 'Course I remember her! She's only been gone for a day- half a day. However long it's been.

SHELLY: Do you remember her when her hair was bright red? Standing in front of an apple tree?

DODGE: What is this, the third degree or something! Who're you to be askin' me personal questions about my wife!

SHELLY: You never look at those pictures up there?

DODGE: What pictures!

SHELLY: You're whole life's up there hanging on the wall. Somebody who looks just like you. Somebody who looks just like you used to look.

DODGE: That isn't me! That never was me! This is me. Right here. This is it. The whole shootin' match, sittin' right in front of you.

SHELLY: So the past never happened as far as you're concerned?

DODGE: The past? Jesus Christ. The past. What do you know about the past?

SHELLY: Not much. I know there was a farm.

Pause

DODGE: A farm?

SHELLY: There's a picture of a farm. A big farm. A bull. Wheat. Corn.

DODGE: Corn?

SHELLY: All the kids are standing out in the corn. They're all waving these big straw hats. One of them doesn't have a hat.

DODGE: Which one was that?

SHELLY: There's a baby. A baby in a woman's arms. The same woman with the red hair. She looks lost standing out there. Like she doesn't know how she got there.

DODGE: She knows! I told her a hundred times it wasn't gonna' be the city! I gave her plenty a' warning.

SHELLY: She's looking down at the baby like it was somebody else's. Like it didn't even belong to her.

DODGE: That's about enough outa' you! You got some funny ideas. Some damn funny ideas. You think just because people propagate they have to love their offspring? You never seen a bitch eat her puppies? Where are you from anyway?

SHELLY: L. A. We already went through that.

DODGE: That's right, L.A. I remember.

SHELLY: Stupid country.

DODGE: That's right! No wonder.

Pause.

SHELLY: What's happened to this family anyway?

DODGE: You're in no position to ask! What do you care? You some kinda' Social Worker?

SHELLY: I'm Vince's friend.

DODGE: Vince's friend! That's rich. That's really rich. "Vince"! "Mr. Vince"! "Mr. Thief " is more like it! His name doesn't mean a hoot in hell to me. Not a tinkle in the well. You know how many kids

I've spawned? Not to mention Grand kids and Great Grand kids and Great Great Grand kids after them?

SHELLY: And you don't remember any of them?

DODGE: What's to remember? Halie's the one with the family album. She's the one you should talk to. She'll set you straight on the heritage if that's what you're interested in. She's traced it all the way back to the grave.

SHELLY: What do you mean?

DODGE: What do you think I mean? How far back can you go? A long line of corpses! There's not a living soul behind me. Not a one. Who's holding me in their memory? Who gives a damn about bones in the ground?

SHELLY: Was Tilden telling the truth?

DODGE *stops short. Stares at* SHELLY. *Shakes his head. He looks off stage left.*

SHELLY: Was he?

DODGE'S *tone changes drastically.*

DODGE: Tilden? *(turns to* SHELLY, *calmly)* Where is Tilden?

SHELLY: Last night. Was he telling the truth about the baby?

Pause.

DODGE: *(turns toward stage left)* What's happened to Tilden? Why isn't Tilden here?

SHELLY: Bradley chased him out.

DODGE: *(looking at* BRADLEY *asleep)* Bradley? Why is he on my sofa? *(turns back to* SHELLY*)* Have I been here all night? On the floor?

SHELLY: He wouldn't leave. I hid outside until he fell asleep.

DODGE: Outside? Is Tilden outside? He shouldn't be out there in the rain. He'll get himself into trouble. He doesn't know his way around here anymore. Not like he used to. He went out West and got himself into trouble. Got himself into bad trouble. We don't want any of that around here.

SHELLY: What did he do?

Pause.

DODGE: *(quietly stares at* SHELLY*)* Tilden? He got mixed up. That's what he did. We can't afford to leave him alone. Not now.

Sound of HALIE *laughing comes from off left.* SHELLY *stands, looking in direction of voice, holding cup and saucer, doesn't know whether to stay or run.*

DODGE: *(motioning to* SHELLY*)* Sit down! Sit back down!

SHELLY *sits. Sound of* HALIE'S *laughter again.*

DODGE: *(to* SHELLY *in a heavy whisper, pulling coat up around him)* Don't leave me alone now! Promise me? Don't go off and leave me alone. I need somebody here with me. Tilden's gone now and I need someone. Don't leave me! Promise!

SHELLY: *(sitting)* I won't.

HALIE *appears outside the screen porch door, up left with* FATHER DEWIS. *She is wearing a bright yellow dress, no hat, white gloves and her arms are full of yellow roses.* FATHER DEWIS *is dressed in traditional black suit, white clerical collar and shirt. He is a very distinguished grey haired man in his sixties. They are both slightly drunk and feeling giddy. As they enter the porch through the screen door,* DODGE *pulls the rabbit fur coat over his head and hides.* SHELLY *stands again.* DODGE *drops the coat and whispers intensely to* SHELLY. *Neither* HALIE *nor* FATHER DEWIS *are aware of the people inside the house.*

DODGE: *(to* SHELLY *in a strong whisper)* You promised!

SHELLY *sits on stairs again.* DODGE *pulls coat back over his head.* HALIE *and* FATHER DEWIS *talk on the porch as they cross toward stage right interior door.*

HALIE: Oh Father! That's terrible! That's absolutely terrible. Aren't you afraid of being punished?

She giggles

DEWIS: Not by the Italians. They're too busy punishing each other.

They both break out in giggles.

HALIE: What about God?

DEWIS: Well, prayerfully, God only hears what he wants to. That's just between you and me of course. In our heart of hearts we know we're every bit as wicked as the Catholics.

They giggle again and reach the stage right door.

HALIE: Father, I never heard you talk like this in Sunday sermon.

DEWIS: Well, I save all my best jokes for private company. Pearls before swine you know.

They enter the room laughing and stop when they see SHELLY. SHELLY *stands.* HALIE *closes the door behind* FATHER DEWIS. DODGE'S *voice is heard under the coat, talking to* SHELLY.

DODGE: *(under coat, to* SHELLY*)* Sit down, sit down! Don't let 'em buffalo you!

SHELLY *sits on stair again.* HALIE *looks at* DODGE *on the floor then looks at* BRADLEY *asleep on sofa and sees his wooden leg. She lets out a shriek of embarrassment for* FATHER DEWIS.

HALIE: Oh my gracious! What in the name of Judas Priest is going on in this house!

She hands over the roses to FATHER DEWIS.

HALIE: Excuse me Father.

HALIE *crosses to* DODGE, *whips the coat off him and covers the wooden leg with it.* BRADLEY *stays asleep.*

HALIE: You can't leave this house for a second without the Devil blowing in through the front door!

DODGE: Gimme back that coat! Gimme back that goddamn coat before I freeze to death!

HALIE: You're not going to freeze! The sun's out in case you hadn't noticed!

DODGE: Gimme back that coat! That coat's for live flesh not dead wood!

HALIE *whips the blanket off* BRADLEY *and throws it on* DODGE. DODGE *covers his head again with blanket.* BRADLEY'S *amputated leg can be faked by having half of it under a cushion of the sofa. He's fully clothed.* BRADLEY *sits up with a jerk when the blanket comes off him.*

HALIE: *(as she tosses blanket)* Here! Use this! It's yours anyway! Can't you take care of yourself for once!

BRADLEY: *(yelling at* HALIE*)* Gimme that blanket! Gimme back that blanket! That's my blanket!

HALIE *crosses back toward* FATHER DEWIS *who just stands there with the roses.* BRADLEY *thrashes helplessly on the sofa trying to reach blanket.* DODGE *hides himself deeper in blanket.* SHELLY *looks on from staircase, still holding cup and saucer.*

HALIE: Believe me, Father, this is not what I had in mind when I invited you in.

DEWIS: Oh, no apologies please. I wouldn't be in the ministry if I couldn't face real life.

He laughs self-consciously. HALIE *notices* SHELLY *again and crosses over to her.* SHELLY *stays sitting.* HALIE *stops and stares at her.*

BRADLEY: I want my blanket back! Gimme my blanket!

HALIE *turns toward* BRADLEY *and silences him.*

HALIE: Shut up Bradley! Right this minute! I've had enough!

BRADLEY *slowly recoils, lies back down on sofa, turns his back toward*

HALIE *and whimpers softly.* HALIE *directs her attention to* SHELLY *again. Pause.*

HALIE: *(to* SHELLY*)* What're you doing with my cup and saucer?

SHELLY: *(looking at cup, back to* HALIE*)* I made some bouillon for Dodge.

HALIE: For Dodge?

SHELLY: Yeah.

HALIE: Well, did he drink it?

SHELLY: No.

HALIE: Did you drink it?

SHELLY: Yes.

HALIE *stares at her. Long pause. She turns abruptly away from* SHELLY *and crosses back to* FATHER DEWIS.

HALIE: Father, there's a stranger in my house. What would you advise? What would be the Christian thing?

DEWIS: *(squirming)* Oh, well. . . . I. . . . I really—

HALIE: We still have some whiskey, don't we?

DODGE *slowly pulls the blanket down off his head and looks toward* FATHER DEWIS. SHELLY *stands.*

SHELLY: Listen, I don't drink or anything. I just—

HALIE *turns toward* SHELLY *viciously.*

HALIE: You sit back down!

SHELLY *sits again on stair.* HALIE *turns again to* DEWIS.

HALIE: I think we have plenty of whiskey left! Don't we Father?

DEWIS: Well, yes. I think so. You'll have to get it. My hands are full.

HALIE *giggles. Reaches into* DEWIS'S *pockets, searching for bottle. She smells the roses as she searches.* DEWIS *stands stiffly.* DODGE *watches* HALIE *closely as she looks for bottle.*

HALIE: The most incredible things, roses! Aren't they incredible, Father?

DEWIS: Yes. Yes they are.

HALIE: They almost cover the stench of sin in this house. Just magnificent! The smell. We'll have to put some at the foot of Ansel's statue. On the day of the unveiling.

HALIE *finds a silver flask of whiskey in* DEWIS'S *vest pocket. She pulls it out.* DODGE *looks on eagerly.* HALIE *crosses to* DODGE, *opens the flask and takes a sip.*

HALIE: *(to* DODGE*)* Ansel's getting a statue, Dodge. Did you know that? Not a plaque but a real live statue. A full bronze. Tip to toe. A basketball in one hand and a rifle in the other.

BRADLEY: *(his back to* HALIE*)* He never played basketball!

HALIE: You shut up, Bradley! You shut up about Ansel! Ansel played basketball better than anyone! And you know it! He was an All American! There's no reason to take the glory away from others.

HALIE *turns away from* BRADLEY, *crosses back toward* DEWIS *sipping on the flask and smiling.*

HALIE: *(to* DEWIS*)* Ansel was a great basketball player. One of the greatest.

DEWIS: I remember Ansel.

HALIE: Of course! You remember. You remember how he could play. *(she turns toward* SHELLY*)* Of course, nowadays they play a different brand of basketball. More vicious. Isn't that right, dear?

SHELLY: I don't know.

HALIE *crosses to* SHELLY, *sipping on flask. She stops in front of* SHELLY.

HALIE: Much, much more vicious. They smash into each other. They knock each other's teeth out. There's blood all over the court. Savages.

HALIE *takes the cup from* SHELLY *and pours whiskey into it.*

HALIE: They don't train like they used to. Not at all. They allow themselves to run amuck. Drugs and women. Women mostly.

HALIE *hands the cup of whiskey back to* SHELLY *slowly.* SHELLY *takes it.*

HALIE: Mostly women. Girls. Sad, pathetic little girls. *(she crosses back to* FATHER DEWIS*)* It's just a reflection of the times, don't you think Father? An indication of where we stand?

DEWIS: I suppose so, yes.

HALIE: Yes. A sort of a bad omen. Our youth becoming monsters.

DEWIS: Well, I uh—

HALIE: Oh you can disagree with me if you want to, Father. I'm open to debate. I think argument only enriches both sides of the question don't you? *(she moves toward* DODGE*)* I suppose, in the long run, it doesn't matter. When you see the way things deteriorate before your very eyes. Everything running down hill. It's kind of silly to even think about youth.

DEWIS: No, I don't think so. I think it's important to believe in certain things.

HALIE: Yes. Yes, I know what you mean. I think that's right. I think that's true. *(she looks at* DODGE*)* Certain basic things. We can't shake certain basic things. We might end up crazy. Like my

husband. You can see it in his eyes. You can see how mad he is.
DODGE *covers his head with the blanket again.* HALIE *takes a single rose from* DEWIS *and moves slowly over to* DODGE.

HALIE: We can't not believe in something. We can't stop believing. We just end up dying if we stop. Just end up dead.

HALIE *throws the rose gently onto* DODGE'S *blanket. It lands between his knees and stays there! Long pause as* HALIE *stares at the rose.* SHELLY *stands suddenly.* HALIE *doesn't turn to her but keeps staring at rose.*

SHELLY: *(to* HALIE*)* Don't you wanna' know who I am! Don't you wanna know what I'm doing here! I'm not dead!

SHELLY *crosses toward* HALIE. HALIE *turns slowly toward her.*

HALIE: Did you drink your whiskey?

SHELLY: No! And I'm not going to either!

HALIE: Well that's a firm stand. It's good to have a firm stand.

SHELLY: I don't have any stand at all. I'm just trying to put all this together.

HALIE *laughs and crosses back to* DEWIS.

HALIE: *(to* DEWIS*)* Surprises, surprises! Did you have any idea we'd be returning to this?

SHELLY: I came here with your Grandson for a little visit! A little innocent friendly visit.

HALIE: My Grandson?

SHELLY: Yes! That's right. The one no one remembers.

HALIE: *(to* DEWIS*)* This is getting a little far fetched.

SHELLY: I told him it was stupid to come back here. To try to pick up from where he left off.

HALIE: Where was that?

SHELLY: Wherever he was when he left here! Six years ago! Ten years ago! Whenever it was. I told him nobody cares.

HALIE: Didn't he listen?

SHELLY: No! No he didn't. We had to stop off at every tiny little meatball town that he remembered from his boyhood! Every stupid little donut shop he ever kissed a girl in. Every Drive-In. Every Drag Strip. Every football field he ever broke a bone on.

HALIE: *(suddenly alarmed, to* DODGE*)* Where's Tilden?

SHELLY: Don't ignore me!

HALIE: Dodge! Where's Tilden gone?

SHELLY *moves violently toward* HALIE.

SHELLY: *(to* HALIE*)* I'm talking to you!

BRADLEY *sits up fast on the sofa,* SHELLY *backs away.*

BRADLEY: *(to* SHELLY*)* Don't you yell at my mother!

HALIE: Dodge! *(she kicks* DODGE*)* I told you not to let Tilden out of your sight! Where's he gone to?

DODGE: Gimme a drink and I'll tell ya'.

DEWIS: Halie, maybe this isn't the right time for a visit.

HALIE *crosses back to* DEWIS.

HALIE: *(to* DEWIS*)* I never should've left. I never, never should've left! Tilden could be anywhere by now! Anywhere! He's not in control of his faculties. Dodge knew that. I told him when I left here. I told him specifically to watch out for Tilden.

BRADLEY *reaches down, grabs* DODGE'S *blanket and yanks it off him. He lays down on sofa and pulls the blanket over his head.*

DODGE: He's got my blanket again! He's got my blanket!

HALIE: *(turning to* BRADLEY*)* Bradley! Bradley, put that blanket back!

HALIE *moves toward* BRADLEY. SHELLY *suddenly throws the cup and saucer against the stage right door.* DEWIS *ducks. The cup and saucer smash into pieces.* HALIE *stops, turns toward* SHELLY. *Everyone freezes.* BRADLEY *slowly pulls his head out from under blanket, looks toward stage right door, then to* SHELLY. SHELLY *stares at* HALIE. DEWIS *cowers with roses.* SHELLY *moves slowly toward* HALIE. *Long pause.* SHELLY *speaks softly.*

SHELLY: *(to* HALIE*)* I don't like being ignored. I don't like being treated like I'm not here. I didn't like it when I was a kid and I still don't like it.

BRADLEY: *(sitting up on sofa)* We don't have to tell you anything, girl. Not a thing. You're not the police are you? You're not the government. You're just some prostitute that Tilden brought in here.

HALIE: Language! I won't have that language in my house!

SHELLY: *(to* BRADLEY*)* You stuck your hand in my mouth and you call me a prostitute!

HALIE: Bradley! Did you put your hand in her mouth? I'm ashamed of you. I can't leave you alone for a minute.

BRADLEY: I never did. She's lying!

DEWIS: Halie, I think I'll be running along now. I'll just put the roses in the kitchen.

DEWIS *moves toward stage left.* HALIE *stops him.*

HALIE: Don't go now, Father! Not now.

BRADLEY: I never did anything, mom! I never touched her! She proposi-
tioned me! And I turned her down. I turned her down flat!

SHELLY *suddenly grabs her coat off the wooden leg and takes both
the leg and coat down stage, away from* BRADLEY.

BRADLEY: Mom! Mom! She's got my leg! She's taken my leg! I never did
anything to her! She's stolen my leg!

BRADLEY *reaches pathetically in the air for his leg.* SHELLY *sets it
down for a second, puts on her coat fast and picks the leg up again.*
DODGE *starts coughing softly.*

HALIE: *(to* SHELLY*)* I think we've had about enough of you young lady.
Just about enough. I don't know where you came from or what
you're doing here but you're no longer welcome in this house.

SHELLY: *(laughs, holds leg)* No longer welcome!

BRADLEY: Mom! That's my leg! Get my leg back! I can't do anything
without my leg.

BRADLEY *keeps making whimpering sounds and reaching for his leg.*

HALIE: Give my son back his leg. Right this very minute!

DODGE *starts laughing softly to himself in between coughs.*

HALIE: *(to* DEWIS*)* Father, do something about this would you! I'm not
about to be terrorized in my own house!

BRADLEY: Gimme back my leg!

HALIE: Oh, shut up Bradley! Just shut up! You don't need your leg now!
Just lay down and shut up!

BRADLEY *whimpers. Lays down and pulls blanket around him. He
keeps one arm outside blanket, reaching out toward his wooden leg.*
DEWIS *cautiously approaches* SHELLY *with the roses in his arms.*
SHELLY *clutches the wooden leg to her chest as though she's kidnapped it.*

DEWIS: *(to* SHELLY*)* Now, honestly dear, wouldn't it be better to try to
talk things out? To try to use some reason?

SHELLY: There isn't any reason here! I can't find a reason for anything.

DEWIS: There's nothing to be afraid of. These are all good people. All
righteous people.

SHELLY: I'm not afraid!

DEWIS: But this isn't your house. You have to have some respect.

SHELLY: You're the strangers here, not me.

HALIE: This has gone far enough!

DEWIS: Halie, please. Let me handle this.

SHELLY: Don't come near me! Don't anyone come near me. I don't need any words from you. I'm not threatening anybody. I don't even know what I'm doing here. You all say you don't remember Vince, okay, maybe you don't. Maybe it's Vince that's crazy. Maybe he's made this whole family thing up. I don't even care any more. I was just coming along for the ride. I thought it'd be a nice gesture. Besides, I was curious. He made all of you sound familiar to me. Every one of you. For every name, I had an image. Every time he'd tell me a name, I'd see the person. In fact, each of you was so clear in my mind that I actually believed it was you. I really believed when I walked through that door that the people who lived here would turn out to be the same people in my imagination. But I don't recognize any of you. Not one. Not even the slightest resemblance.

DEWIS: Well you can hardly blame others for not fulfilling your hallucination.

SHELLY: It was no hallucination! It was more like a prophecy. You believe in prophecy, don't you?

HALIE: Father, there's no point in talking to her any further. We're just going to have to call the police.

BRADLEY: No! Don't get the police in here. We don't want the police in here. This is our home.

SHELLY: That's right. Bradley's right. Don't you usually settle your affairs in private? Don't you usually take them out in the dark? Out in the back?

BRADLEY: You stay out of our lives! You have no business interfering!

SHELLY: I don't have any business period. I got nothing to lose.

She moves around, staring at each of them.

BRADLEY: You don't know what we've been through. You don't know anything!

SHELLY: I know you've got a secret. You've all got a secret. It's so secret in fact, you're all convinced it never happened.

HALIE *moves to* DEWIS

HALIE: Oh, my God, Father!

DODGE: *(laughing to himself)* She thinks she's going to get it out of us. She thinks she's going to uncover the truth of the matter. Like a detective or something.

BRADLEY: I'm not telling her anything! Nothing's wrong here! Nothin's ever been wrong! Everything's the way it's supposed to be! Nothing ever happened that's bad! Everything is all right here! We're all good people!

DODGE: She thinks she's gonna suddenly bring everything out into the open after all these years.

DEWIS: *(to* SHELLY*)* Can't you see that these people want to be left in peace? Don't you have any mercy? They haven't done anything to you.

DODGE: She wants to get to the bottom of it. *(to* SHELLY*)* That's it, isn't it? You'd like to get right down to bedrock? You want me to tell ya'? You want me to tell ya' what happened? I'll tell ya'. I might as well.

BRADLEY: No! Don't listen to him. He doesn't remember anything!

DODGE: I remember the whole thing from start to finish. I remember the day he was born.

Pause

HALIE: Dodge, if you tell this thing—if you tell this, you'll be dead to me. You'll be just as good as dead.

DODGE: That won't be such a big change, Halie. See this girl, this girl here, she wants to know. She wants to know something more. And I got this feeling that it doesn't make a bit a' difference. I'd sooner tell it to a stranger than anybody else.

BRADLEY: *(to* DODGE*)* We made a pact! We made a pact between us! You can't break that now!

DODGE: I don't remember any pact.

BRADLEY: *(to* SHELLY*)* See, he doesn't remember anything. I'm the only one in the family who remembers. The only one. And I'll never tell you!

SHELLY: I'm not so sure I want to find out now.

DODGE: *(laughing to himself)* Listen to her! Now she's runnin' scared!

SHELLY: I'm not scared!

DODGE *stops laughing, long pause.* DODGE *stares at her.*

DODGE: You're not huh? Well, that's good. Because I'm not either. See, we were a well established family once. Well established. All the boys were grown. The farm was producing enough milk to fill Lake Michigan twice over. Me and Halie here were pointed toward what looked like the middle part of our life. Everything was settled with us. All we had to do was ride it out. Then Halie got pregnant again. Outa' the middle a' nowhere, she got pregnant. We weren't planning on havin' any more boys. We had enough boys already. In fact, we hadn't been sleepin' in the same bed for about six years.

HALIE: *(moving toward stairs)* I'm not listening to this! I don't have to listen to this!

DODGE: *(stops* HALIE*)* Where are you going! Upstairs! You'll just be listenin' to it upstairs! You go outside, you'll be listenin' to it outside. Might as well stay here and listen to it.

HALIE *stays by stairs*

BRADLEY: If I had my leg you wouldn't be saying this. You'd never get away with it if I had my leg.

DODGE: *(pointing to* SHELLY*)* She's got your leg. *(laughs)* She's gonna keep your leg too. *(to* SHELLY*)* She wants to hear this. Don't you?

SHELLY: I don't know.

DODGE: Well even if ya' don't I'm gonna' tell ya'. *(pause)* Halie had this kid. This baby boy. She had it. I let her have it on her own. All the other boys I had had the best doctors, best nurses, everything. This one I let her have by herself. This one hurt real bad. Almost killed her, but she had it anyway. It lived, see. It lived. It wanted to grow up in this family. It wanted to be just like us. It wanted to be a part of us. It wanted to pretend that I was its father. She wanted me to believe in it. Even when everyone around us knew. Everyone. All our boys knew. Tilden knew.

HALIE: You shut up! Bradley, make him shut up!

BRADLEY: I can't.

DODGE: Tilden was the one who knew. Better than any of us. He'd walk for miles with that kid in his arms. Halie let him take it. All night sometimes. He'd walk all night out there in the pasture with it. Talkin' to it. Singin' to it. Used to hear him singing to it. He'd make up stories. He'd tell that kid all kinds a' stories. Even when he knew it couldn't understand him. Couldn't understand a word he was sayin'. Never would understand him. We couldn't let a thing like that continue. We couldn't allow that to grow up right in the middle of our lives. It made everything we'd accomplished look like it was nothin'. Everything was cancelled out by this one mistake. This one weakness.

SHELLY: So you killed him?

DODGE: I killed it. I drowned it. Just like the runt of a litter. Just drowned it.

HALIE *moves toward* BRADLEY

HALIE: *(to* BRADLEY*)* Ansel would've stopped him! Ansel would've stopped him from telling these lies! He was a hero! A man! A whole man! What's happened to the men in this family! Where are the men!

Suddenly VINCE *comes crashing through the screen porch door up left, tearing it off its hinges. Everyone but* DODGE *and* BRADLEY *back away from the porch and stare at* VINCE *who has landed on his stomach on the porch in a drunken stupor. He is singing loudly to himself and hauls himself slowly to his feet. He has a paper shopping bag full of empty booze bottles. He takes them out one at a time as he sings and smashes them at the opposite end of the porch, behind the solid interior door, stage right.* SHELLY *moves slowly toward stage right, holding wooden leg and watching* VINCE.

VINCE: *(singing loudly as he hurls bottles)* "From the Halls of Montezuma to the Shores of Tripoli. We will fight our country's battles on the land and on the sea."

He punctuates the words "Montezuma", "Tripoli", "battles" and "sea" with a smashed bottle each. He stops throwing for a second, stares toward stage right of the porch, shades his eyes with his hand as though looking across to a battle field, then cups his hands around his mouth and yells across the space of the porch to an imaginary army. The others watch in terror and expectation.

VINCE: *(to imagined Army)* Have you had enough over there! 'Cause there's a lot more here where that came from! *(pointing to paper bag full of bottles)* A helluva lot more! We got enough over here to blow ya' from here to Kingdomcome!

He takes another bottle, makes high whistling sound of a bomb and throws it toward stage right porch. Sound of bottle smashing against wall. This should be the actual smashing of bottles and not tape sound. He keeps yelling and heaving bottles one after another.

VINCE *stops for a while, breathing heavily from exhaustion. Long silence as the others watch him.* SHELLY *approaches tentatively in* VINCE'S *direction, still holding* BRADLEY'S *wooden leg.*

SHELLY: *(after silence)* Vince?

VINCE *turns toward her. Peers through screen.*

VINCE: Who? What? Vince who? Who's that in there?

VINCE *pushes his face against the screen from the porch and stares in at everyone.*

DODGE: Where's my goddamn bottle!

VINCE: *(looking in at* DODGE*)* What? Who is that?

DODGE: It's me! Your Grandfather! Don't play stupid with me! Where's my two bucks!

VINCE: Your two bucks?

HALIE *moves away from* DEWIS, *upstage, peers out at* VINCE, *trying to recognize him.*

HALIE: Vincent? Is that you, Vincent?

SHELLY *stares at* HALIE *then looks out at* VINCE.

VINCE: *(from porch)* Vincent who? What is this! Who are you people?

SHELLY: *(to* HALIE*)* Hey, wait a minute. Wait a minute! What's going on?

HALIE: *(moving closer to porch screen)* We thought you were a murderer or something. Barging in through the door like that.

VINCE: I am a murderer! Don't underestimate me for a minute! I'm the Midnight Strangler! I devour whole families in a single gulp!

VINCE *grabs another bottle and smashes it on the porch.* HALIE *backs away.*

SHELLY: *(approaching Halie)* You mean you know who he is?

HALIE: Of course I know who he is! That's more than I can say for you.

BRADLEY: *(sitting up on sofa)* You get off our front porch you creep! What're you doing out there breaking bottles? Who are these foreigners anyway! Where did they come from?

VINCE: Maybe I should come in there and break them!

HALIE: *(moving toward porch)* Don't you dare! Vincent, what's got into you! Why are you acting like this?

VINCE: Maybe I should come in there and usurp your territory!

HALIE *turns back toward* DEWIS *and crosses to him.*

HALIE: *(to* DEWIS*)* Father, why are you just standing around here when everything's falling apart? Can't you rectify this situation?

DODGE *laughs, coughs.*

DEWIS: I'm just a guest here, Halie. I don't know what my position is exactly. This is outside my parish anyway.

VINCE *starts throwing more bottles as things continue.*

BRADLEY: If I had my leg I'd rectify it! I'd rectify him all over the goddamn highway! I'd pull his ears out if I could reach him!

BRADLEY *sticks his fist through the screening of the porch and reaches out for* VINCE, *grabbing at him and missing.* VINCE *jumps away from* BRADLEY'S *hand.*

VINCE: Aaaah! Our lines have been penetrated! Tentacles animals! Beasts from the deep!

VINCE *strikes out at* BRADLEY'S *hand with a bottle.* BRADLEY *pulls his hand back inside.*

SHELLY: Vince! Knock it off will ya'! I want to get out of here!

VINCE *pushes his face against screen, looks in at* SHELLY.

VINCE: *(to* SHELLY*)* Have they got you prisoner in there, dear? Such a sweet young thing too. All her life in front of her. Nipped in the bud.

SHELLY: I'm coming out there, Vince! I'm coming out there and I want us to get in the car and drive away from here. Anywhere. Just away from here.

SHELLY *moves toward* VINCE'S *saxophone case and overcoat. She sets down the wooden leg, downstage left and picks up the saxophone case and overcoat.* VINCE *watches her through the screen.*

VINCE: *(to* SHELLY*)* We'll have to negotiate. Make some kind of a deal. Prisoner exchange or something. A few of theirs for one of ours. Small price to pay if you ask me.

SHELLY *crosses toward stage right door with overcoat and case.*

SHELLY: Just go and get the car! I'm coming out there now. We're going to leave.

VINCE: Don't come out here! Don't you dare come out here!

SHELLY *stops short of the door, stage right.*

SHELLY: How come?

VINCE: Off limits! Verboten! This is taboo territory. No man or woman has ever crossed the line and lived to tell the tale!

SHELLY: I'll take my chances.

SHELLY *moves to stage right door and opens it.* VINCE *pulls out a big folding hunting knife and pulls open the blade. He jabs the blade into the screen and starts cutting a hole big enough to climb through.*

BRADLEY *cowers in a corner of the sofa as* VINCE *rips at the screen.*

VINCE: *(as he cuts screen)* Don't come out here! I'm warning you! You'll disintegrate!

DEWIS *takes* HALIE *by the arm and pulls her toward staircase.*

DEWIS: Halie, maybe we should go upstairs until this blows over.

HALIE: I don't understand it. I just don't understand it. He was the sweetest little boy!

DEWIS *drops the roses beside the wooden leg at the foot of the staircase then escorts* HALIE *quickly up the stairs.* HALIE *keeps looking back at* VINCE *as they climb the stairs.*

HALIE: There wasn't a mean bone in his body. Everyone loved Vincent. Everyone. He was the perfect baby.

DEWIS: He'll be all right after a while. He's just had a few too many that's all.

HALIE: He used to sing in his sleep. He'd sing. In the middle of the night. The sweetest voice. Like an angel. *(she stops for a moment.)* I used to lie awake listening to it. I used to lie awake thinking it was all right if I died. Because Vincent was an angel. A guardian angel. He'd watch over us. He'd watch over all of us.

DEWIS *takes her all the way up the stairs. They disappear above.* VINCE *is now climbing through the porch screen onto the sofa.* BRAD-LEY *crashes off the sofa, holding tight to his blanket, keeping it wrapped around him.* SHELLY *is outside on the porch.* VINCE *holds the knife in his teeth once he gets the hole wide enough to climb through.* BRADLEY *starts crawling slowly toward his wooden leg, reaching out for it.*

DODGE: *(to* VINCE*)* Go ahead! Take over the house! Take over the whole goddamn house! You can have it! It's yours. It's been a pain in the neck ever since the very first mortgage. I'm gonna die any second now. Any second. You won't even notice. So I'll settle my affairs once and for all.

As DODGE *proclaims his last will and testament,* VINCE *climbs into the room, knife in mouth and strides slowly around the space, inspecting his inheritance. He casually notices* BRADLEY *as he crawls toward his leg.* VINCE *moves to the leg and keeps pushing it with his foot so that it's out of* BRADLEY'S *reach then goes on with his inspection. He picks up the roses and carries them around smelling them.* SHELLY *can be seen outside on the porch, moving slowly center and staring in at* VINCE. VINCE *ignores her.*

DODGE: The house goes to my Grandson, Vincent. All the furnishings, accoutrements and parapernalia therein. Everything tacked to the walls or otherwise resting under this roof. My tools—namely my band saw, my skill saw, my drill press, my chain saw, my lathe, my electric sander, all go to my eldest son, Tilden. That is, if he ever shows up again. My shed and gasoline powered equipment, namely my tractor, my dozer, my hand tiller plus all the attachments and riggings for the above mentioned machinery, namely my spring tooth harrow, my deep plows, my disk plows, my automatic fertiliz-ing equipment, my reaper, my swathe, my seeder, my John Deere Harvester, my post hole digger, my jackhammer, my lathe—(to himself) Did I mention my lathe? I already mentioned my lathe— my Bennie Goodman records, my harnesses, my bits, my halters, my brace, my rough rasp, my forge, my welding equipment, my shoeing nails, my levels and bevels, my milking stool—no, not my milking stool—my hammers and chisels, my hinges, my cattle gates, my barbed wire, self-tapping augers, my horse hair ropes and all related materials are to be pushed into a gigantic heap and set ablaze in the very center of my fields. When the blaze is at its highest, preferably on a cold, windless night, my body is to be pitched into the middle of it and burned til nothing remains but ash.

Pause. VINCE *takes the knife out of his mouth and smells the roses. He's facing toward audience and doesn't turn around to* SHELLY. *He folds up knife and pockets it.*

SHELLY: *(from porch)* I'm leaving, Vince. Whether you come or not, I'm leaving.

VINCE: *(smelling roses)* Just put my horn on the couch there before you take off.

SHELLY: *(moving toward hole in screen)* You're not coming?

VINCE *stays downstage, turns and looks at her.*

VINCE: I just inherited a house.

SHELLY: *(through hole, from porch)* You want to stay here?

VINCE: *(as he pushes* BRADLEY'S *leg out of reach)* I've gotta carry on the line. I've gotta see to it that things keep rolling.

BRADLEY *looks up at him from floor, keeps pulling himself toward his leg.* VINCE *keeps moving it.*

SHELLY: What happened to you Vince? You just disappeared.

VINCE: *(pause, delivers speech front)* I was gonna run last night. I was gonna run and keep right on running. I drove all night. Clear to the Iowa border. The old man's two bucks sitting right on the seat beside me. It never stopped raining the whole time. Never stopped once. I could see myself in the windshield. My face. My eyes. I studied my face. Studied everything about it. As though I was looking at another man. As though I could see his whole race behind him. Like a mummy's face. I saw him dead and alive at the same time. In the same breath. In the windshield, I watched him breathe as though he was frozen in time. And every breath marked him. Marked him forever without him knowing. And then his face changed. His face became his father's face. Same bones. Same eyes. Same nose. Same breath. And his father's face changed to his Grandfather's face. And it went on like that. Changing. Clear on back to faces I'd never seen before but still recognized. Still recognized the bones underneath. The eyes. The breath. The mouth. I followed my family clear into

Iowa. Every last one. Straight into the Corn Belt and further. Straight back as far as they'd take me. Then it all dissolved. Everything dissolved.

SHELLY *stares at him for a while then reaches through the hole in the screen and sets the saxophone case and* VINCE'S *overcoat on the sofa. She looks at* VINCE *again.*

SHELLY: Bye Vince.

She exits left off the porch. VINCE *watches her go.* BRADLEY *tries to make a lunge for his wooden leg.* VINCE *quickly picks it up and dangles it over* BRADLEY'S *head like a carrot.* BRADLEY *keeps making desperate grabs at the leg.* DEWIS *comes down the staircase and stops half way, staring at* VINCE *and* BRADLEY. VINCE *looks up at* DEWIS *and smiles. He keeps moving backwards with the leg toward upstage left as* BRADLEY *crawls after him.*

VINCE: *(to* DEWIS *as he continues torturing* BRADLEY) Oh, excuse me Father. Just getting rid of some of the vermin in the house. This is my house now, ya' know? All mine. Everything. Except for the power tools and stuff. I'm gonna get all new equipment anyway. New plows, new tractor, everything. All brand new. *(VINCE teases* BRADLEY *closer to the up left corner of the stage.)* Start right off on the ground floor.

VINCE *throws* BRADLEY'S *wooden leg far off stage left.* BRADLEY *follows his leg off stage, pulling himself along on the ground, whimpering. As* BRADLEY *exits* VINCE *pulls the blanket off him and throws it over his own shoulder. He crosses toward* DEWIS *with the blanket and smells the roses.* DEWIS *comes to the bottom of the stairs.*

DEWIS: You'd better go up and see your Grandmother.

VINCE: *(looking up stairs, back to* DEWIS) My Grandmother? There's nobody else in this house. Except for you. And you're leaving aren't you?

DEWIS *crosses toward stage right door. He turns back to* VINCE.

DEWIS: She's going to need someone. I can't help her. I don't know what to do. I don't know what my position is. I just came in for some tea. I had no idea there was any trouble. No idea at all.

VINCE *just stares at him.* DEWIS *goes out the door, crosses porch and exits left.* VINCE *listens to him leaving. He smells roses, looks up the staircase then smells roses again. He turns and looks upstage at* DODGE. *He crosses up to him and bends over looking at* DODGE'S *open eyes.* DODGE *is dead. His death should have come completely blanket, then covers his head. He sits on the sofa, smelling roses and staring at* DODGE'S *body. Long pause.* VINCE *places the roses on* DODGE'S *chest then lays down on the sofa, arms folded behind his head, staring at the ceiling. His body is in the same relationship to* DODGE'S. *After a while* HALIE'S *voice is heard coming from above the staircase. The lights start to dim almost imperceptibly as* HALIE *speaks.* VINCE *keeps staring at the ceiling.*

HALIE'S VOICE: Dodge? Is that you Dodge? Tilden was right about the corn you know. I've never seen such corn. Have you taken a look at it lately? Tall as a man already. This early in the year. Carrots too. Potatoes. Peas. It's like a paradise out there, Dodge. You oughta' take a look. A miracle. I've never seen it like this. Maybe the rain did something. Maybe it was the rain.

As HALIE *keeps talking off stage,* TILDEN *appears from stage left, dripping with mud from the knees down. His arms and hands are covered with mud. In his hands he carries the corpse of a small child at chest level, staring down at it. The corpse mainly consists of bones wrapped in muddy, rotten cloth. He moves slowly downstage toward the staircase, ignoring* VINCE *on the sofa.* VINCE *keeps staring at the ceiling as though* TILDEN *wasn't there. As* HALIE'S VOICE *continues,* TILDEN *slowly makes his way up the stairs. His eyes never leave the corpse of the child. The lights keep fading.*

HALIE'S VOICE: Good hard rain. Takes everything straight down deep to the roots. The rest takes care of itself. You can't force a thing to grow. You can't interfere with it. It's all hidden. It's all unseen. You just gotta wait til it pops up out of the ground. Tiny little shoot. Tiny little white shoot. All hairy and fragile. Strong though. Strong enough to break the earth even. It's a miracle, Dodge. I've never seen a crop like this in my whole life. Maybe it's the sun. Maybe that's it. Maybe it's the sun.

TILDEN *disappears above. Silence. Lights go to black.*

SEDUCED

Seduced was first produced at the American Place Theater in New York City. It was directed by Jack Gelber with the following cast:

Henry Hackamore: Rip Torn
Raul: Ed Setrakian
Luna: Pamela Reed
Miami: Carla Borelli

ACT 1

SCENE:

In the dark, Randy Newman's song SAIL AWAY *from the album of the same name (Reprise) is heard over the sound system. Very slowly, in the tempo of the song, the lights start to come up on stage. The stage is basically bare and empty but for two lone palm trees, each one situated at the extreme downstage left and right corners of the playing area, not in the apron. They are very lush, well cared for trees about seven feet tall and each planted in a large, black clay Mexican pot. The entire upstage wall is covered from floor to ceiling by a jet black velour curtain which can be mechanically raised until it's unseen in the flies above. Dead center stage is an old black naugahyde reclining chair which resembles a dentist's chair. It's raised off the ground about a foot. The chair is situated horizontally on stage with the head toward stage left.* HENRY HACKAMORE *is seen lying flat out on the chair as the lights come up. He is naked except for a baggy pair of white boxer shorts with a draw string. His hair is shoulder length and white, long white beard, long cork-screw shaped fingernails and toe-nails. He is old to the point of looking ancient. His body is extremely thin and emaciated. The general impression is a cross between a prisoner of war and an Indian fakir. As the song continues,* HENRY *slowly extracts single sheets of Kleenex from a large box on a night stand beside his chair and slowly spreads the sheets on different parts of his body, starting with his feet and working toward his chest. He continues this action over and over until the song ends. The song ends and* HENRY'S *attention seems to be pulled toward the palm tree in the down right corner. He moves himself up to a more vertical position on his elbows and scrutinizes the tree. He squints his eyes. He pulls himself up even more. The sheets of Kleenex flutter to the floor.*

HENRY: *(sitting up, looking hard at palm tree down right; calling to someone off)* Raul!

RAUL *enters quickly from left. A heavy set, middle-aged man, dark hair. Wears a brightly colored Hawaiian print shirt with a black shoulder holster and snub-nosed .38 over the top of the shirt. White pants, black shoes. He crosses to the bed beside* HENRY

RAUL: Sir?

HENRY: Don't "sir" me. *(pointing to palm down right)* You can see the state of the palm. Without even looking. You can feel that something's off.

RAUL *looks at the palm and then back to* HENRY

RAUL: It's out of place sir?

HENRY: Out of place! It's off the deep end! Look at the position it's in! Do something about it.

RAUL: Yes sir.

RAUL *crosses down right to the palm and squats down, prepared to turn the base to suit* HENRY

HENRY: What are you doing! Why are you squatting down like a Filipino house boy! I didn't ask for that.

RAUL *stands quickly*

RAUL: I'm sorry sir.

HENRY: Can't you see what's called for. Can't you perceive it on your own without me guiding you every step of the way. Take a step back. Step away from it!

RAUL *steps back from the palm and looks at it, then looks back at* HENRY

HENRY: There. Now look. Can't you tell now.

RAUL: I'm not sure what you want sir.

HENRY: What *I* want? What I want is for you to know instinctively what I want. Without any coaching. Without hints. For you to be living inside the very rhythm of my needs.

RAUL *moves to the palm tree and turns it slightly.*

HENRY: Now what are you doing! Put it back! Put it back like it was!

RAUL *turns the palm back to its original position*

HENRY: That's not it! That's not it. It's getting worse. I can't believe it.

RAUL *keeps turning the palm trying to restore it to its original position*

HENRY: After all these years! Still out of touch. Get away from the damn thing! Stand back away from it!

RAUL *stands back from the palm*

HENRY: Now just look at it. Just stand there and look at it.

RAUL: I am sir.

HENRY: Now try to see it in relationship to the space around it. Try to see the space it's consuming.

RAUL: I am.

HENRY: Now try to see the space it's not consuming. Can you see that?

Long pause as RAUL *stares at the palm*

HENRY: No, you can't see that. See? That's where it goes wrong. All right, all right. I was asking too much. I was pushing it. I was hoping that after so many years you might have picked up a trick or two but I can see I was mistaken.

RAUL: I'm willing to try sir.

HENRY: Trying's not enough. Just forget it.

RAUL: If you just describe to me how you want it, I'll move it.

HENRY: No! Descriptions don't describe the picture I have in my head. I need some turning now. Come and turn me.

RAUL: *(Moving to* HENRY*)* Yes sir.

HENRY: Left side first. Left side.

RAUL *moves to the upstage side of the chair and rolls* HENRY *onto his left side and holds him in that position as* HENRY *speaks*

HENRY: We'll have to get a palm specialist in here. Probably hard to find in this country.

RAUL: Oh, I don't think so sir. We could dig one up.

HENRY: No Americans, though. That's what we need. An American to deal with it. Someone who understands the urgency. Down here they have a different sense of time or something. Things go on forever without getting done.

RAUL: We could fly one in.

HENRY: Never mind. I'll deal with it later. I'll have you walk me over to it.

RAUL: No walking, sir.

HENRY: Don't keep repeating my limitations to me as though I've forgotten. As long as I've got them I can't forget them. *(pause)* Rock me. Back and forth.

RAUL *gently rocks his body back and forth, still keeping* HENRY *on his left side.*

HENRY: Oh, that is stupendous! What a motion! Suddenly I'm flooded with wonderful pictures.

RAUL: Of what, sir?

HENRY: Of this place. Of the outside. Of how the outside must find us. This is a new place, isn't it?

RAUL: Yes sir.

HENRY: Of course it is. A new place in a series of new places. A stepping stone. You're trying to sneak me back in, isn't that it? Didn't I give orders to that effect?

RAUL: We're trying to get you closer to the border, sir. In case of an emergency.

HENRY: Closer? The women are still coming though?

RAUL: Oh yes, sir.

HENRY: That's still in the plan.

RAUL: Yes sir.

HENRY: *(Still being rocked)* I've got to see them. Every last one of them. Oh, these women, Raul! Wait til you see them! Fifteen years it's been. Wait til you see the way they carry themselves. Like visions. Like moving pictures. How are they coming?

RAUL: Jet, sir.

HENRY: Individually?

RAUL: Yes sir.

HENRY: We have that many planes left?

RAUL: I think so.

HENRY: Good. Do my feet. My feet.

RAUL: Jet, sir.

RAUL *rolls* HENRY *onto his back*

HENRY: Move me up first. Pull me up!

RAUL: Yes sir.

RAUL *moves to the head of the chair, grabs* HENRY *under the arms and pulls him up to a semi-sitting position. He props pillows behind his back, then moves down to* HENRY'S *feet and starts massaging his toes.* HENRY *keeps talking*

HENRY: Pictures, Raul. Pictures! Every shift of the body brings a new wave. It's amazing. Almost a rejuvenating effect, although I shouldn't go overboard in my expectations. *(pause)* We came here at night, didn't we?

RAUL: Yes sir.

HENRY: Always at night. Pitch black. Wrapped in a grey stretcher. Theoretically I shouldn't have seen a thing. Numb to the world.

RAUL: There was a full moon.

HENRY: I was asleep?

RAUL: You'd awake in fits.

HENRY: Fits?

RAUL: Spurts.

HENRY: Oh yeah. Short bursts. Short bursts of waking. Still, that doesn't account for these vivid details. Golden beaches. Black-headed kids. Shimmering, silver water. How do you account for that?

RAUL: You're seeing that now?

HENRY: Off and on. It must come from the touching. Do my feet.

RAUL: I am, sir.

HENRY: You are? You're doing them now?

RAUL: Yes sir.

HENRY: That's funny. I can't feel a thing.

RAUL: Well, it comes and goes, doesn't it sir?

HENRY: That's right. Comes and goes. Can't depend on it. But why all those images then?

RAUL: we could raise the curtain.

HENRY *jerks his feet away from* RAUL *and struggles to a sitting position.* RAUL *tries to calm him.*

HENRY: No! Nothing from out there comes in here! Nothing! No life! Not sun, not moon, not sound, not nothing!

RAUL: I know, sir. I'm sorry.

HENRY: That's the law! That's the absolute law!

RAUL: I know, sir.

HENRY: What a suggestion! Curtain up in the middle of the day.

RAUL: I just thought you might want it for a second. A minute or two.

HENRY: Stop trying to make your desires mine. If you need a vacation it can be arranged. Don't piddle around in here trying to figure out what's best for you in the disguise of what's best for me. We've been together too long for that.

RAUL: I just thought if you were seeing things it might be good to open up the room a little.

HENRY: I'm always seeing things! The room's got nothing to do with it. I was seeing things before you were born. Before I was born I was seeing things. I prefer seeing things to having them crash through my window in the light of day. It's a preference not a disappointment.

RAUL: *(Pause)* Would you like something to eat, sir?

HENRY: *(Pause)* Why do you always do that? Why do you constantly switch the areas of my concern? Food is not on my mind. Food has nothing to do with what's on my mind. Pictures are on my mind and you put food in there. They don't mix! Pictures of food don't mix!

RAUL: I'm sorry sir.

HENRY: You have to be more sensitive, Raul, to the subtle shifts in my intellectual activity. The mind covers a wide range of territory. Sometimes simultaneously traveling several different hemispheres in a single sweep and then diving suddenly for the prey.

RAUL: I understand, sir.

HENRY: You do? You understand what the prey is? The prey is an idea. A single, lonely, fleeting idea trying to duck into a rabbit hole and the mind comes sweeping in for the kill.

RAUL: It's a beautiful idea sir.

HENRY: That's not an idea! It's a description. An idea is something useful. *(pause)* Do my back. My back!

RAUL *moves around to the head of the chair and starts massaging* HENRY'S *back. Pause*

RAUL: It would be great to fly over America in the daytime though. Just once. Somewhere over Nevada.

HENRY: Where did that idea come from? Out of the clear blue sky. Flying? What an idea.

RAUL: Just to see it. I haven't seen it in ten years.

HENRY: That's not true. Anyway, nothing's changed. I guarantee it. All it would do is tempt you. Fill you with a lot of aching. Desire again. Desire all over the place. Land of lust.

RAUL: These women—

HENRY: What about them?

RAUL: I'm not to touch them. You don't have to worry about that.

HENRY: Something in your need to remind me, fills me with trepidation. You should take it for granted that you won't touch them.

RAUL: I do, sir.

HENRY: Don't take it as a taboo. That will only lead to trouble. It should be deeply rooted in your blood.

RAUL: What should?

HENRY: Your lack of lust! Haven't you learned anything from me! I should be a living testimony. Of course it would help if I was living more. More alive. Nevertheless you should be able to see where desire leads just by looking. That not only goes for the body, Raul, but the spirit, the soul. The body's the least of it.

RAUL: *(Still massaging)* I can't see your soul, sir.

HENRY: Of course not. Good point. But take it from me, there are certain unseen parts that are thoroughly ravaged beyond recognition. Worse than what you see. Far worse.

RAUL: Can you feel my hands?

HENRY: Vaguely. Keep rubbing.

RAUL: Yes sir.

HENRY: *(Pause)* I want you to keep something in mind, Raul. When these women begin to fill up my room I want you to keep something firmly in mind.

RAUL: Yes sir.

HENRY: I want you to constantly remember, as you're taking them in with your eyes, that at one time or another I've penetrated every single one of them. Every last one. Right to the core. Straight to the heart.

RAUL: I will sir.

HENRY: Promise?

RAUL: I'm not to touch them sir. You can be sure of that.

HENRY *violently pulls himself away from* RAUL'S *touch.*

HENRY: Stop saying that! Stop telling me that!

RAUL: Should I leave, sir?

HENRY: No!

RAUL: Should I take a vacation?

HENRY: No vacation! Not at this point in the game. I might need you at any minute. At any minute we may have to evacuate. You're aware of that.

RAUL: Yes sir.

Pause. HENRY *looks hard at* RAUL

HENRY: You're more aware of it than I am in fact. That's why you've brought me here. Closer to the border. My lucidity is not without its bounds, Raul. It comes and goes like the rest of it. But that's no reason to assume that I'm a total blathering fool. Crisis is a normal state of affairs. Emergency is the seed of great decisions. I'm not blind to the fact of my dying. I'm living it while you're on the outskirts. While you're hanging around in a holding pattern dreaming about America in the daylight. While asshole doctors visit me in my sleep. Sneaking in here in the dark and shaking their heads over my bed. Waiting across the border for me, in a hospital I built myself with excess cash.

RAUL: No one's gone over your head sir. No decisions without your approval.

HENRY: That's obvious! The decisions are mine! It's a fool-proof organization although at times I wonder how it could be when the very ones closest to me seem farthest away.

RAUL: You are the sole stockholder, sir.

HENRY: Your forthrightness fills me with suspicion, Raul. Now why should that be? How could that be the case? Has my body poisoned my mind along with everything else? Why does it seem like every nuance in your verbal patterns is designed to hide some sneaky truth? Like you're standing there watching me through a one-way mirror when I can see you plain as day. It is you, isn't it? *(suddenly panics, screaming)* RAUL! IT IS YOU ISN'T IT?

RAUL *rushes to him and holds him firmly.* HENRY *grabs onto his arms in terror.* RAUL *strokes his head and calms him down.*

RAUL: *(Stroking his head)* Yes sir. It's me. It's always me.

HENRY: Rub my head! My head!

RAUL *eases him back into the pillows, rubbing his head.*

RAUL: Try to be calm sir.

HENRY: Calm? Have you ever known terror to be calm?

RAUL: No sir.

HENRY: Don't let them take me while I'm sleeping, Raul. Promise me.

RAUL: I won't, sir.

HENRY: Even if they think I'm dead I won't be.

RAUL: No sir.

HENRY: I'll just be sleeping.

RAUL: Yes sir.

HENRY: Last time they took me while I slept.

RAUL: It was your orders, sir.

HENRY: My orders?

RAUL: Yes sir.

HENRY: Where do my orders come from, Raul?

Pause as RAUL *strokes his head.*

RAUL: Would you like a drink sir?

HENRY: What is there?

RAUL: Pineapple, coconut, papaya, mango, tangelo.

HENRY: A paradise. America never had such things. Not the America I knew.

RAUL: Oh, I'm sure they have all the juices up there by now sir.

HENRY: I'm sure. If I didn't travel by night I'd see some of these things.

RAUL: You might.

HENRY: I'd see more than I bargained for probably. *(Pause.)* Why is daylight so terrifying, Raul?

RAUL: I don't know.

HENRY: Pineapple. Make it pineapple. Pineapple seems the least dangerous.

RAUL: Yes sir. *(Moving away from* HENRY*)* Try to sleep if you can.

HENRY: Don't be stupid.

RAUL *exits stage left.* HENRY *lies there a while silently. He starts to
sing to himself, repeating the same phrase over and over again.*

HENRY: *(singing to himself)* Hey ba ba re bop. Hey ba ba re bop. Hey
ba ba re bop. Hey ba ba re bop.

*He stops singing and sits up abruptly in the chair. He looks around
the space as though remembering something then carefully gets up
and pulls out a large cardboard box from underneath the reclining
chair. He next pulls out a roll of paper towels and starts tearing off
sections and laying them on the floor. He starts singing again as he
does this, repeating the phrase.*

HENRY: *(singing)* Hey ba ba re bop. Hey ba ba re bop. *(etc.)*

*He sits on the floor and pats the towels firmly then pulls out several
thick manuscripts from the cardboard box. He picks up each one and
pounds it on all four edges on top of the paper towels, examines the
edges for straightness then stacks them neatly on the floor beside the
box. He goes through this process like a private ritual which has lost
its original purpose. As he continues repeating this action while singing, the large black curtain upstage begins to slowly ascend up into
the flies revealing a slightly raised platform. As the curtain continues
to rise, without* HENRY'S *knowing, venetian blinds are revealed which
cover the entire upstage wall from floor to ceiling. The blinds are open
and through the cracks can be seen a huge silver full moon with a long
reflection cast on what appears to be the ocean. Directly in front of
the blinds, standing on the platform, upstage center is a beautiful
young woman named* LUNA. *She has black hair and is dressed like
a Hollywood starlet of the 30's. Furs, high heels, stockings with seams,
patent leather purse, etc. She just stands there looking down at*
HENRY *until the black curtain has disappeared above.* HENRY *continues with his manuscripts and singing, unaware of her presence. His
back is always to her. She speaks from the platform.*

HENRY: *(Singing)* Hey ba ba re bop. Hey ba ba re bop. *(etc.)*

LUNA: *(From the platform)* So, the real Henry Hackamore is taking
guests?

HENRY *stops singing immediately and struggles to his feet but does
not turn upstage to see her. His body seems unable to turn around.*

He scrambles for a brass bell underneath the reclining chair. He pulls it out and starts ringing it frantically for help and calling RAUL. LUNA *stays on the platform and smiles down at him.*

HENRY: *(Ringing the bell.)* Raul! We've been penetrated! They've found their way in!

LUNA: *(giggling but staying behind him on platform)* Visitors from the outside world. Alien life.

HENRY: *(ringing bell)* Raul! Drop the pineapple and get in here!

HENRY *drops the bell and starts frantically putting all the manuscripts back into the cardboard box and shoves it under the chair.*

LUNA: Sweeping it under the table Henry? You are the real Henry, aren't you?

HENRY: *(ringing bell again)* RAUL!

HENRY *keeps scrambling with the manuscripts, cleaning up the paper towels.*

LUNA: I'd hate to have come all this way to be in the company of a stranger.

RAUL *charges on from left with his pistol drawn. He sees* LUNA *and stops. He looks at* HENRY *and then puts his gun back in the holster.*

HENRY: *(To* RAUL*)* Where have you been! There's someone in here! Right now, there's someone in here! I can't see them but I hear them!

RAUL: It's one of the ladies, sir.

HENRY: What ladies! Help me up on the chair! Help me!

RAUL *goes to* HENRY *and lifts him onto the chair so that he's facing front with his back to* LUNA, *legs hanging over the side. He starts pulling sheets of kleenex out of the box and covering his legs with them.*

RAUL: *(as he helps* HENRY*)* One of the guests.

HENRY: There are no guests, only visitors!

RAUL: She's a visitor then, sir.

HENRY: How did she get in!

LUNA *giggles and walks back and forth on the platform.*

RAUL: I don't know sir.

HENRY: Ask her!

RAUL: *(to* LUNA*)* Mr. Hackamore would like to know how you got in, mam?

LUNA: It wasn't easy.

RAUL: *(to* HENRY*)* She won't give a straight answer sir.

HENRY: Well get her around here in front of me for God's sake! I can't see through the back of my head.

RAUL: *(To* LUNA*)* Mr. Hackamore is unable to turn around, mam. Could you come down here in front of him so he can see you?

LUNA: Mr. Hackamore is unable to turn around?

RAUL: Yes mam.

LUNA: He can hear me, can't he? Isn't that enough? He doesn't have to see me. He hasn't seen me for fifteen years. Why stop now?

HENRY: Who is this one? I don't like the sound of her.

RAUL: *(to* LUNA*)* Could you tell Mr. Hackamore your name?

LUNA: Oh, he knows my name. Just leave us alone. You're very charming but unnecessary. I'm not going to hurt him. I'm just teasing him a little.

HENRY: I can't stand this!

LUNA: He's getting excited.

RAUL: *(to* HENRY*)* Try not to scream, sir.

HENRY: Why won't she come around here! Raul, use your influence.

RAUL *moves upstage toward* LUNA. *She stops him.*

LUNA: *(to* RAUL*)* Easy. Easy. I'm not alone.

HENRY: She was told to come alone! Everything's falling apart.

LUNA: *(to* RAUL*)* Just go away and leave us. I'll be nice to him. Don't worry.

HENRY: *(still facing front)* Don't leave, Raul! Not until I see her face.

RAUL: Please mam. All you have to do is let Mr. Hackamore see you and then I'll go.

HENRY: Is she beautiful, Raul?

RAUL: Yes sir.

HENRY: Very beautiful?

RAUL: Yes sir.

HENRY: You're not getting worked up, are you?

RAUL: No sir.

HENRY: You're remembering what I told you?

RAUL: Yes sir.

LUNA: *(to* RAUL*)* You two have an agreement, is that it?

HENRY: Don't talk to her, Raul! Don't get involved.

LUNA *laughs*

RAUL: Please, mam.

LUNA: Oh, don't beg me. You can see I'm harmless.

RAUL: I can't leave him alone.

LUNA: All right. All right. I'll reveal myself. Slowly. A step at a time. *She starts to move slowly off the platform, down toward* HENRY *as she speaks.*

RAUL: She's coming sir.

HENRY: Wonderful!

LUNA: Anticipation is delicious, isn't it Henry? Truly delicious. The best part in fact.

HENRY: I recognize this line of thinking.

RAUL: You know her now, sir?

HENRY: Not yet.

LUNA: *(to* HENRY*)* Isn't your whole body thundering? Mine is.

HENRY: Oh God, Raul! What'd I tell you! Didn't I tell you this would be terrific!

RAUL: Do you want me to leave you now sir?

HENRY: No! There's still a possible danger. There's always that slim chance of danger. Just when you let your guard down.

LUNA: It's true. That's when it happens. Just when you let your guard down.

HENRY: It's almost worth the risk, though.

LUNA: *(still advancing, coming left toward* HENRY *from behind)* This *is* risky, Henry. Very risky.

HENRY: I don't care. I've been in jams before. Jams of an international stature. This is nothing.

LUNA: Peanuts.

HENRY: Just come around so I can see you! Just show yourself!

LUNA: Easy, Henry.

HENRY: Don't make a fool out of me in front of my bodyguard!

LUNA: Oh, please Henry. It's you that won't let him go. All this could be avoided.

RAUL: I'll turn around sir.

HENRY: Yes! Yes, turn around. Cover your eyes. Plug up your ears. This is between me and myself.

RAUL *turns around upstage right and covers his eyes.* LUNA *keeps advancing. She comes up almost parallel with* HENRY. *Stage left of him.*

LUNA: Silly. It's very silly.

HENRY: It's not silly! It's desperate. Show yourself!

LUNA *suddenly walks out directly in front of* HENRY *and smiles at him. She opens her furs. She is wearing a slinky blue evening gown, diamond necklace and earrings. She lets the furs fall to her elbows and turns herself seductively in front of him like a high fashion model. Henry stares in awe.*

HENRY: Oh God. Oh my living God. Oh my Christ. Raul, did you see this? Don't look!

RAUL *drops his hands from his eyes then quickly covers them again.*

HENRY: *(stretching his hand out toward* LUNA*)* Oh.

LUNA *moves toward him, smiling and reaches for his hand.* HENRY *pulls it back quickly.*

LUNA: You are a demon, Henry.

HENRY: I was.

LUNA: Anyone with nails like that should have been dead long ago. What're you raising, cork screws or something?

HENRY: Rub my head.

She moves toward him. HENRY *pulls back*

HENRY: No!

RAUL: Can I leave now, sir?

HENRY: Yes. No! Wait a minute. *(to* LUNA*)* Empty your purse out.

LUNA: Henry, this is insulting. It's not enough that I liquidate my affairs over night after not hearing from you for years, leave without telling a soul my destination in an unmarked jet, for an unmarked island but on top of it all I have to empty my purse out on your bed?

HENRY: Do it.

LUNA *rips open her purse and dumps the contents on the chair beside* HENRY, *to his right.*

HENRY: Raul, check it.

RAUL *moves to the chair and looks through the objects quickly*

RAUL: It's all right sir.

HENRY: Nothing that could be construed as a weapon?

RAUL: Nothing.

HENRY: No daggers? Poison? Bombs? Even the most innocent looking things are potential killers.

RAUL: No sir. She's clean.

HENRY: Good. Put the contents in a plastic bag. Take the bag to the parking lot. Drive the Chevrolet back and forth over the bag sixteen times. Collect the smashed remains and put them in another bag. Take that bag to the beach. Rent a small boat. Row out to the twenty mile limit. Dump the bag. Abandon the boat and swim to shore.

RAUL: *(starts to move)* Yes sir.

HENRY: Oh, before you do that bring us in a chaise longue and two tall drinks.

RAUL: Yes sir.

RAUL sweeps the objects off the chair into his shirt and exits left. LUNA watches RAUL. HENRY watches her.

HENRY: *(after pause)* Don't be insulted. Everyone gets the same treatment. Some are even flattered.

LUNA: Flattered?

HENRY: Yes, flattered. The innocent crave to be guilty. There's a certain pride in having one's dormant criminal instincts beckoned up by suspicion. It's not even that I'm particularly suspicious.

LUNA: Just cautious.

HENRY: Just careful.

LUNA: Just nuts. That was harmless stuff. A bunch of harmless make-up!

HENRY: Nothing's harmless til it's squashed.

LUNA: If you expect this meeting to go on for any length of time you might try lightening up your act, Henry.

HENRY: I'm sorry but I don't even know you.

LUNA: That's it!

She moves as if to go then stops when HENRY speaks.

HENRY: No please! I thought I'd recognize you immediately but it's taking some time. You are beautiful though.

LUNA: Thanks.

HENRY: There'll be something for you to sit on in a minute. I don't like keeping anything extra in here. Just more surfaces for things to collect on. Microscopic things. That's the worst. What you can't see. I'd have you sit on my chair—*(pauses.)* Just a minute.

He starts pulling off sections of paper towel and spreading them on the chair beside him.

LUNA: Don't worry about it. I like standing.

HENRY: *(continuing with towels)* Did you like the plane?

LUNA: The plane?

HENRY: The jet. I designed it from scratch. The very latest.

LUNA: Yes, it's fine.

HENRY: It's yours. You can take it back with you.

LUNA: Thanks.

HENRY: Were you expecting more?

LUNA: Look, Henry. Just relax, all right? I'm here out of curiosity more than anything else. Don't jump to conclusions.

HENRY: Sorry.

LUNA: I have a life already. I don't need more.

HENRY: Good. One of the satisfied. One of the few.

RAUL *pushes on a green and white striped bamboo chaise longue from stage left. He pushes it across the stage behind* HENRY'S *chair and places it down right facing left. He exits left again.*

HENRY: There we are. Just in the nick of time. Bamboo. My favorite, bamboo. *(to* LUNA*)* Now you won't have to sit on my chair after all. You won't have to deposit unseen, invisible plant life.

He pushes all the paper towels onto the floor and slaps his hands together. LUNA *smiles at the chaise longue then looks at* HENRY.

LUNA: *(looking at chaise)* If I sit does that mean I'm staying?

HENRY: You want to stay, don't you? You wouldn't have come if you didn't want to stay.

LUNA: You don't seem to have any trouble staying. How long have you been here anyway?

HENRY: None of that stuff!

LUNA: Too sticky, huh? Too filled with reverberations? I could be working for anyone now, right?

HENRY: You're still on the payroll.

LUNA: Are you kidding? You think I've been sitting there by the pool, waiting for your next whim all these years?

HENRY: Don't tell me about it! Times have changed. I've lived through earthquakes, disasters, corruptions, fall-out, wives, losses beyond belief.

LUNA: Poor baby.

HENRY: I don't need that! I'm not responsible now for your naive beliefs in what I was then. Anything I might have told you was a lie.

LUNA: True.

HENRY: So why needle me?

LUNA: Then you do recognize me? You do remember?

HENRY: I remember something. Parts of something.

LUNA: You're lucky I still recognize *you.*

HENRY: I'm sorry. I didn't have a chance to clean up. We lost track of the planes.

LUNA: Planes? You mean there's other ones coming?

HENRY *pauses*

LUNA: There are, aren't there? Same old shit as it always was. All the "dollies."

HENRY: I've been in the company of men for twenty one years and in all that time I've never raised my voice so much as I have in the past ten minutes!

LUNA: *(in sex-kitten voice)* I'm sorry, Henry. Let me comply. Anything you want. Just tell me. Tell me once and it's yours.

HENRY: Anything?

LUNA: The world.

HENRY: I have that.

LUNA: Something else?

HENRY: What else is there?

LUNA: Heaven?

HENRY: Oh, my God!

LUNA: Heaven, Henry?

HENRY: You're being sarcastic! It's uncanny how you lose touch with female elusiveness.

LUNA: I'm not, Henry. I'm not now and I wasn't then.

HENRY: Wasn't what! My mind's a jumble from all this.

LUNA: Sarcastic.

HENRY: Oh.

LUNA: I'm not. Anything you want.

HENRY: Don't confuse my body. My mind can take it but not the body.

LUNA: Are you actually dying, Henry?

HENRY: I suppose. I suppose I actually am. They tell me I'm actually not but actually I am. I know it. They wouldn't have moved me here if I wasn't. I look it, don't I?

LUNA: You look like something from another world.

HENRY: I am. That's true. I can't take the sun anymore.

LUNA: Do you want me to rub you like I used to?

HENRY: No! I have a man for that! Nothing from outside touches me! Go sit down!

LUNA *goes down right and sits on the chaise, facing toward* HENRY. *She preens herself, pulls her dress up and crosses her legs.*

HENRY: *(struggling to get up from chair)* It's a mutual arrangement. I don't touch it, it doesn't touch me. That's what happens when you rape something, isn't it?

LUNA: Rape?

HENRY: Yes! Rape. After that you don't touch. There's a repulsion between both sides.

LUNA: I wouldn't know.

HENRY: Really? That clean, huh? That above it all?

LUNA: Don't fall, Henry.

HENRY: *(still struggling to stand)* I'm not falling! I'm standing! There's certain machinery at work that thinks I can't even move. Some even think I'm dead. Others don't know. Most others don't know. That's the best of all. Keeping them all in the dark. That's the best.

LUNA stretches herself out on the chaise as HENRY tries to walk inch by inch toward her.

LUNA: Like me?

HENRY: You're the least of it. Harmless. The worst is invisible. They know that. That's why they fear me. That's why they can't put a finger on me. A stab in the dark.

LUNA: Are you coming toward me Henry?

LUNA stretches herself seductively for him. Henry inches his his way toward her.

HENRY: *(trying to walk)* They comb the cities for me. Little American towns. Fortunes are spent on hired assassins. Presidents fear me. International Secret Agencies, Internal Revenues. Secretaries of Defense. Mobsters. Gang Lords, Dictators, Insurance Detectives. None of them can touch me. None of them.

LUNA: *(stretching, arms over her head)* You're a master, Henry. A wizard!

HENRY: I'm invisible!

LUNA: *(giggling)* I can see you.

HENRY: Untouchable!

LUNA: *(Holding out her arms to him)* Touch me.

HENRY tries painfully to get closer to her. Puts out his arm

HENRY: I can't.

LUNA: Can you see me, Henry? Look.

She rolls herself from side to side.

HENRY: Something. Something's there.

LUNA: What do you see?

She rakes her fingers through her hair and lets it fall over the chaise.

HENRY: I see you moving.

LUNA: Keep watching.

HENRY: I am.

She writes on the chaise as HENRY *keeps getting nearer.*

LUNA: Do you see me breathing?

HENRY: Yes! I see your skin moving. It's incredible.

She arches her back & smiles at him

LUNA: Do you see my teeth?

HENRY: Yes! Your teeth. Your pearly gates.

LUNA: What else?

HENRY: Your femaleness. It's an awesome power.

LUNA *squirms with delight.* HENRY *is getting closer to her.*

LUNA: Henry, it's only me.

HENRY: It's not only you! It's a force. With men I was always a master. They'd lick my heels. Men become dogs in a second. It's the female that's dangerous. Uncontrollable. Cat-like.

LUNA: Henry.

She runs her hands over her stomach and hip.

HENRY: Your pearly gates. Look at them spreading for me. Shining. Calling me in. It's exactly how I pictured it. Exactly. The gates of heaven! You were right.

LUNA: I was?

Her actions get more and more erotic

HENRY: They never counted on this. My private salvation. My ultimate acquisition. No spy in the world could ever see what I really had my eyes on. Where my real hunger lay. My ravenous appetite. Beyond private holdings. My instincts were right. At the front door to death I needed women! Women more than anything! Women to fill me up. To ease me into the other world. To see me across. To bring me ecstacy and salvation! Don't let me fall! Don't ever let me fall!

HENRY *collapses on top of* LUNA *and goes unconscious.* LUNA *screams and tries to struggle out from under him but he stays laying across her.* RAUL *rushes on from left with two tall tropical-looking drinks. He sees the situation and puts the drinks down on the night table beside* HENRY'S *chair. He rushes over to* HENRY *and* LUNA *on the chaise.*

LUNA: Get him off of me! Get him off!

RAUL: Mr. Hackamore!

LUNA: Jesus Christ!

RAUL *sweeps* HENRY *up in his arms and rushes him over to his chair and lays him down.* LUNA *stands and brushes herself off.*

LUNA: If he thinks I flew all the way down here to get jumped on, he's crazy.

RAUL: *(to LUNA as he attends HENRY)* How did this happen! What've you been doing to him?

LUNA: Me? I didn't do a damn thing! He collapsed on me. Started mumbling about salvation and ecstacy, next thing I knew, wham, he's on top of me. The guy's a maniac.

RAUL turns away from HENRY and approaches LUNA slowly. She backs up from him slightly.

RAUL: I want to tell you something, mam. You haven't seen the boss in fifteen years, right?

LUNA: Yeah. So what?

RAUL: In fifteen years a lot of things happen. A whole lot of things. Now he may have invited you down here for some reason. But whatever that reason is it don't mean shit on shinola if it gets in our way. You understand?

LUNA: I think so.

RAUL: I think so too. Now you just string him along with whatever he wants. He may want a lot of funny things but you just play the ball game. Just like all the rest of us. We've been doing it for all these years. It won't hurt you to do it for a few days.

LUNA: A few days?

RAUL: Maybe less. Don't worry, it won't be that long.

RAUL turns and exits left. LUNA is left alone with HENRY who is still unconscious, breathing heavily. She crosses up to him slowly and looks at him. She reaches out to touch him then pulls her hand away.

LUNA: Henry?

No response from HENRY

LUNA: Henry, don't die, O.K.?

HENRY stays unconscious. MIAMI enters from up right on the upstage platform, looking out through the blinds then down toward LUNA. She is a voluptuous young blonde woman dressed in the same style and era as LUNA but in pale orange and salmon colors. The effect of both women should be that they've stepped directly out of HENRY'S past without aging. She crosses downstage toward HENRY and LUNA.

MIAMI: *(to LUNA)* Cripes, how many floors they got in this crib? I come up twenty-five on the elevator and the lights go blank. No numbers. Thing's still shootin up. Pickin up speed. Feel like to puke.

LUNA: *(motioning to drinks)* Have a drink.

MIAMI: *(taking off her coat)* You kidding? That'd do it for sure. That'd put it right over the top. I gotta get my sea legs first. *(looks at* HENRY*)* Who's this old dude?

LUNA: Don't you recognize him?

MIAMI *tosses her coat over* HENRY'S *legs and takes a closer look at him.*

MIAMI: Am I supposed to? Looks like he's half dead.

LUNA: He is. At least half.

*(*LUNA *picks up a drink and crosses back down right to the chaise and sits.* MIAMI *moves around* HENRY'S *chair.)*

MIAMI: Weird place to die in, if he's dyin.

LUNA: He's dying, all right.

MIAMI: Somethin about your tone of voice gives me the feelin that you know somethin more than me. I don't like that feelin.

LUNA: Tough.

MIAMI: Nasty.

LUNA: I can back it up.

MIAMI: Hold it, hold it. I'm still in the grips of jet-lag. I'm not here for a slug out. I've got an appointment.

LUNA: *(laughing)* An appointment!

MIAMI: For some reason I had the idea I was gonna be met with bowls of roses. Little guys dressed up like Phillip Morris relieving me of my wrap.

LUNA: Well, there's nothing like disappointment for broadening one's character.

MIAMI: Hey, look, don't use words like "one's" around me, o.k.? Gives me the creeps. Just talk like a person. I mean if we're gonna be spendin any time together.

LUNA: I doubt if we will be.

MIAMI: Swell. What is this, the waiting room or something?

LUNA: What's your name?

MIAMI: Miami.

LUNA: Miami, this is not the waiting room. This is *the* room. The main room. The inner-most chamber room. The secret nucleus that everything springs from. The Pharaoh's crypt. And lying in state, at the very heart of things, is the Pharaoh himself.

MIAMI: *(pointing to* HENRY*)* He's the Pharaoh?

LUNA: He's the Hackamore. *The* Mr. Henry Malcolm Hackamore.

MIAMI *looks at* HENRY *then back to* LUNA *then crosses closer to* HENRY *and takes another look.*

MIAMI: No shit. This is him, huh?

LUNA: The one and only.

MIAMI: Whew! Got a little unravelled, didn't he?

LUNA: He's let himself go.

MIAMI: I'll say. I don't know if I can handle this.

MIAMI *picks up the other drink and takes a sip.*

LUNA: This is nothing. Wait til he wakes up.

RAUL *enters from left pushing an intra-venous rack with a bottle of blood hanging upside down and a long tube attached.* MIAMI *backs off down left and watches as* RAUL *inserts the needle in* HENRY'S *arm and tapes it down.* MIAMI *looks over to* LUNA *who shrugs her shoulders.* HENRY *suddenly speaks but stays still. The women listen.*

HENRY: Raul?

RAUL: Yes sir.

HENRY: That's you?

RAUL: Yes sir.

HENRY: Whose blood is it this time?

RAUL: Only the best sir. Guaranteed.

HENRY: Genius blood? Only genius blood?

RAUL *looks uneasily at the women then answers* HENRY.

RAUL: Yes sir. Only genius.

HENRY: Good. Because I've made my decision.

RAUL: What's that sir?

HENRY: To fly. I'm going to fly again.

RAUL: Fly sir?

HENRY: Straight to Nevada. I'm going to land in Nevada in the middle of the day. I'm going to land with my women. All of us. We're going to disembark in the blazing sun. We're going to appear out of nowhere. We're going to climb into sixteen black Chevrolets and drive straight out across the Mojave desert.

RAUL: You think you're capable of flying again sir?

The women move in closer to the couch to hear HENRY.

HENRY: I'm capable of anything. At any moment anything is possible. Now I want you to find me the proper equipment. The jacket I used to wear. The helmet. The scarf. I'll need all those things.

RAUL: Yes sir.

HENRY: *(noticing curtain is up)* And lower the damn curtain! How long has it been up like that?

RAUL: Not long sir.

HENRY: Lower it! Anything could be out there trying to get in.

HENRY: Anything! Have you got any idea what's out there, Raul? Any idea at all?

RAUL: No sir.

HENRY: The world at large! That's what's out there. Wild. Un-dominated. Ravenous for the likes of us. Ready to gobble us up at the drop of a hat. We can't allow penetration. Not at any cost. Whatever the price we have to pay it to insure our immunity. You have to insure that for me, Raul. It's in your hands. These women will deliver me. These two women. Nobody else. I don't want anybody else in here.

RAUL: Nobody's getting in here sir.

HENRY: *(to himself as he lies back on chair)* This time I'll escape for good. It's guaranteed. A clean sweep. A slice of the atom. Cataclysmic. Perfect timing. Absolutely perfect timing.

HENRY *beckons the women toward him. They start to move very slowly and hesitatingly toward* HENRY. *Randy Newman's song* Lonely at the Top *from the* Sail Away *album (Reprise Records) comes on over the sound system. The big black curtain upstage starts to slowly descend, covering the blinds, moon, etc. The descent of the curtain is very slow and timed to touch the stage floor just as the song ends. The stage lights are fading in the same tempo as the curtain.* HENRY *keeps slowly beckoning the women toward him. Song ends. Lights go to black.* RAUL *exits.*

ACT 2

SCENE:

In the dark, Randy Newman's You Can Leave Your Hat On *From the* Sail Away *album is heard. Lights come up on stage. The big black curtain is down.* HENRY *is seated on his chair facing front to audience, legs hanging over the side. He is rubbing his entire body with alcohol from a bottle on the night stand. He seems to be entirely absorbed in this process and continues in a slow rhythmical way in time to the music. The two women are standing upstage facing the audience.* MIAMI *to stage right,* LUNA *to stage left. They each have on a lush fur coat. A small black chair is beside each of them. They move seductively to the music.* HENRY *stays front without turning around to them. They follow the instructions in the song and each let their coats fall to their elbows then drop them to the floor. They pick up their chairs and move downstage in time to the music. They set their chairs downstage right and left then they each take off their dress and let it fall to the floor.* LUNA *mimes the line in the song about turning off the light. They both stand on the chairs. They don't take off their high heels as the song suggests. All they are wearing is bra, panties, garter belts, silk stockings with seams, black high heels and whatever jewelry they had on. They raise their arms up above their heads and move to the music.* HENRY *keeps rubbing himself with the alcohol. Now and then he looks up at the two women but his gaze seems indifferent. After the verse which ends, "You give me reason to live,"* HENRY *gets up from the chair with the bottle of alcohol and moves downstage center looking at the women and rubbing his arms. He crosses slowly to each of them through the last verse as they keep undulating to the music.* HENRY *crosses back up center to his chair and sits again facing the audience as the song ends. He keeps rubbing himself as the women get down off the chairs and put their dresses back on.*

HENRY: *(as women dress)* Very impressive. Very interesting little rendition. Choice of music's a little off the wall but aside from that I'd say you two make a nifty combination.

LUNA: Thanks Henry. You were always more than generous.

HENRY: I was never more than generous! I was never guilty enough to be more than generous.

MIAMI: Henry, what's the scoop here anyway? What've you got planned for us?

HENRY: Planned? *(laughs to himself)* You girls believe in destiny don't ya? To a certain extent? Prophecy of one kind or another?
The women look at each other then back to HENRY.

HENRY: I mean you're not gonna tell me that you map out every move you make in a day. Calculate your every word. There's still a spark of the sense of adventure left? Am I wrong?

MIAMI: It's always good to see you Henry.

HENRY: That's right. I've never let you down in the past.

LUNA: Well—

HENRY: Well what!

LUNA: Maybe once.

HENRY: When was that? You're not gonna drag up a lot a' dreary reminiscences for me now are ya'? A lot a' false accusations over circumstances beyond your control!

LUNA: Beyond *my* control?

HENRY: And mine! Certain moves had to be made. Without hesitation! Certain disclosures. Immediate decisions.

LUNA: All right! It's too far gone now anyway.

HENRY: Don't play magnanimous with me!

LUNA: Well, shall we go tooth and nail with it then, Henry? Shall we really get into it?

MIAMI: *(crossing to* LUNA*)* Look, let's not go and get worked up about the past, okay?

HENRY: She started it! She's the one!

LUNA: *(laughing)* Henry, you're wonderful! You're absolutely wonderful! I always felt like I was ten years old around you and I still do.

HENRY: I'll resist the temptation to take that as a slur. My visions were always of you reveling in the luxury of hotel rooms. Sinking up to the neck in bubble baths. Blanketing your naked body with Pomeranians. All at my expense!

LUNA: *(laughing)* Yes! That was me! That was me!

HENRY: Hardly the environment that would foster complaint! Let alone accusations. You, high on the hog and me, risking my life in a desert junkyard!

LUNA: *(laughing harder)* Oh! Risking your life! Yes! For me!

HENRY: That's right! Shadow-boxing with the underground isn't my idea of a kid's game. There was danger at every turn!

LUNA: *(still laughing)* Danger!

MIAMI: Knock it off will ya'! *(*LUNA *stops laughing.)* Jesus, I didn't fly all the way down here to get treated to this.

HENRY *goes silent, starts pulling out sheets of kleenex and putting them on his legs. Pause.*

MIAMI: Henry?

HENRY *stays silent, absorbed in the kleenex action.* MIAMI *and* LUNA *look at each other.*

MIAMI: *(crossing to* HENRY*)* Henry, look, it's all right with me if you want to keep this thing a secret. I'm game. It's kind of exciting not knowing what to expect. *(*HENRY *stays silent with kleenex)* We don't want to upset you or anything. I'm just a little curious about why you asked us down here. That's all.

LUNA: I don't think he even remembers.

MIAMI: *(to* HENRY*)* Sure he remembers. Don't you Henry? Didn't you say you wanted to take us flying?

HENRY *looks up at her. Pause.*

HENRY: *(stares into space)* There was a song about that.

MIAMI: A song?

HENRY: A silver plane.

MIAMI: What song was that, Henry?

HENRY *goes back to putting kleenex on his legs.*

HENRY: *(referring to* LUNA*)* She knows what song it was. She used to try to sing it. Used to think she was a singer. Even had me convinced. Spent a lot a' money on that voice.

MIAMI: *(to* LUNA*)* You remember a song?

LUNA: Not me. Musta' been one of his rural discoveries. One of his quaint little waitress-types.

HENRY: Turns out she could only sing two lines. That's all she could memorize. Two lines.

MIAMI: I could sing something for you if you want me to.

HENRY: You? *(looks at* MIAMI*)* You can't sing, can ya'?

MIAMI: Sure.

HENRY: You can't sing a note. I remember you. You could barely even talk.

MIAMI: *(moving away from him)* Boy, Henry, you really are a pisser! You know that? A real charmer.

HENRY: Okay, go ahead and sing something. Thrill me.

MIAMI: I think the moment's past! All the inspiration went right out the window!

HENRY: *(laughs)* Inspiration! That's great! Inspiration. Well, that's what ya' get for relying on inspiration, sister!

LUNA: Henry, is this going to be just another opportunity for you to indulge in insults? What do you want from us? Here we are. You sent for us and here we are. I'm not willing to hang around here while you bombard us with your twisted little versions of injury. I didn't even know you were still alive until I got your telegram.

HENRY: *(smiling to* LUNA*)* There's still no way to be sure about that, is there?

Long pause. LUNA *stares at him. He stares back.*

LUNA: Well, you're not are you? Henry, don't try to scare me, all right? This situation is already getting me a little bit on edge. I think you owe us some kind of an explanation.

HENRY: That'd be nice, wouldn't it. A little explanation. That'd be real nice. I tell ya' what. We'll have an exchange. You do a little explaining then I'll do a little explaining. Stroke for stroke. That way none of us will be left out on a limb.

LUNA: Well there's nothing to explain. You know all about me already.

MIAMI: What do you wanna' know from us?

HENRY: I want to know what it's been like.

MIAMI: What what's been like?

Pause

HENRY: Life. Living. That's simple enough, isn't it?

LUNA: Life in general, you mean?

HENRY: No. Life in particular. What it smells like. What it tastes like. What it sounds like.

LUNA: Jesus Christ.

HENRY: That's not so unusual, is it?

LUNA: You mean you've been that cut off all these years?

HENRY *suddenly goes back to the kleenex and starts putting it on his legs again. The women move in toward him.*

LUNA: *(after pause)* Henry, I'm sorry. I'll tell you anything you want to know.

HENRY *quickly looks up at* MIAMI.

HENRY: What about her?

LUNA: What *about* her?

HENRY: I need a commitment! A pact. We all have to come into agreement. It's no good if two of us is willing and the third one isn't. It's the third one that always spoils everything! It's the third one that stabs you in the back! That's the one you have to watch out for!

MIAMI: I agree already!

HENRY: It's no good just saying it. The words mean nothing. The words just fly out and disappear into thin air. *(to* LUNA*)* Isn't that right?

LUNA: Yes. I guess so.

HENRY: You're not sure. If you're not sure we can't proceed. You have to be absolutely sure. You have to be convinced beyond a shadow of a doubt! We have to be in communion. Completely in communion!

LUNA: All right! What do you want, a contract!

HENRY: *(short pause)* A contract.

LUNA: Maybe we should all slash our wrists and drink each other's blood or something! I mean how far do you want to carry this thing?

HENRY: A contract sounds good. I'll agree to that.

The women look at each other and stifle a laugh.

LUNA: All right, Henry. Let's make a contract. You got a piece of paper or something?

HENRY: Paper's filthy! I don't keep the stuff around.

LUNA: *(moving toward his manuscripts under chair)* You've got papers underneath your chair there.

HENRY: You stay away from that! *(LUNA stops)* Just stay away! That's no concern of yours.

LUNA *backs away.*

MIAMI: Henry, maybe we could skip the contract thing.

HENRY: No! *(to MIAMI)* See, it's you! You! You're the one! You're the one who wants to stifle the project! Turn around in fifty years and you'll be sittin' at the head of the table! That's the way you'd like it, isn't it? A flimsy verbal agreement. That way you can manipulate and twist things up any way you like. Well, I'm not puttin' one cent into this thing unless we have a contract.

LUNA: And we can't have a contract unless we have paper!

HENRY: Write it in the air!

LUNA: *(short pause)* What?

HENRY: Write it in the air.

The women break into laughter.

HENRY: Shut up! *(They stop laughing.)* Neither one of ya's got the sense God gave a chicken! City girls. Couple a' dumb-ass city girls. You laugh at air! You think air's funny, huh? Well I happen to have built an entire legacy on nothin' but air!

Silence

HENRY: That's right. Thin air. Invisible. Tiny little invisible molecules. Jet propulsion! Whad'ya' think about that? The wings of a plane? *He stretches his arms out horizontally and slowly tips them from side to side. He smiles at the women.*

HENRY: Now, what happens when a thing moves through space? What happens?

He lowers his arms very slowly. The women seem almost hypnotized by his movements now.

HENRY: Do you see anything? Do you see anything leaving a trail? A path? a ghost? A memory of the movement? It's all being recorded. Isn't that something? It's all being left behind and you can't even see it.

His arms finally come to rest at his sides.

HENRY: Put your hand out in front of you. Your finger.

LUNA *stretches her right arm with her finger pointed in front of her.*

HENRY: Both of you!

MIAMI *does the same.*

HENRY: That's right. Now—write the words. Write the words I tell you. In plain English. Bold print. I want to see the letters speak. Write this: "We agree—". Write! "We agree—".

The women write simultaneously in the air. HENRY *squints to make out the invisible letters.*

HENRY: That's right. "This day." Go ahead. Write, "This day—".

The women continue writing the words in the air. HENRY *watches closely.*

HENRY: "We agree—this day—to everything." Write that! "To everything."

The women finish writing the sentence.

HENRY: Good. Now sign it. Both of you.

They sign their names in the air.

HENRY: Now each of you sign the other one's.

They look at him, not understanding.

HENRY: As a witness! Countersign it! Go ahead.

They switch places and sign their names again.

HENRY: Good. Now I'll put my sign here.

HENRY *makes a strange writing mark in mid air and dots it.*

HENRY: There. Now that was painless, wasn't it? Perfunctory and painless. These things have to be taken care of. Now we can breathe a little more freely. Now that we know we're protected.

LUNA: Henry, do you think we could get something to drink? I'm feeling a little bit dizzy.

HENRY: Drink? We don't have anything to celebrate yet. A contract's nothing to celebrate. I never went in for that stuff.

MIAMI: All right, let's get this over with. What do you want us to do now?

HENRY: That's not the attitude. This has to be a voluntary endeavor, otherwise it won't work.

LUNA: Couldn't we raise the curtain or something? It's so claustrophobic in here. I don't know how you stand it.

HENRY: The curtains? No! It's too distracting.

LUNA: Just to get a little sunlight in here.

HENRY: No! *(pause)* This is no vacation! I didn't call ya' down here just to dress up the furniture. There's plenty a' others I could've called for that. You don't seem to recognize the importance of this meeting. You two are my last link. My very last possibility.

MIAMI: For what?

HENRY: For remembering. For bringing something back. Raul's no good for that anymore. I used to depend on him. He used to give me regular reports. But now he's gone sour. I need a woman's version. Two women. Two is always better than one. Now let's start with Las Vegas. That's as good a place to start as any. How 'bout it?

MIAMI: Vegas? *(She looks at LUNA)*

HENRY: Yeah. What'sa' matter with Vegas?

MIAMI: I haven't been to Vegas since nineteen fifty-two.

HENRY: *(to LUNA)* What about you?

LUNA: *(to HENRY)* The last time I was there it was with you.

HENRY: Me? You were never there with me! I woulda' remembered that.

LUNA: Henry, this is going nowhere fast. Can't we play cards or something?

HENRY: No! There's no time for cards! I'm not lookin' for diversions! What'sa' matter with you two? Maybe you don't have any experience. Nothin'. Nothin' to relate. Is that it? A couple a' zombies?

MIAMI: All right. Las Vegas, 1952.

HENRY: You don't have anything more recent, huh?

MIAMI: Well, yeah. Sure. I got uh-New Orleans. I got some good Memphis stories. St. Louis. Take your pick.

HENRY: Vegas.

MIAMI: Vegas it is.

HENRY: It has to be Vegas. *(pointing downstage right, by palm)* Go down there and tell it. Down there. I wanna' see you in the proper setting.

MIAMI: By the tree?

HENRY: Right. By the tree. *(to LUNA)* You come here. Come here and stand next to me. Over here. That's right.

LUNA *crosses to* HENRY, *stands next to him.*

HENRY: *(to* LUNA*)* Not too close.

LUNA *moves slightly away from* HENRY, MIAMI *has crossed down right to the palm tree.*

HENRY: *(to* MIAMI*)* Move a little bit to your left. *(*MIAMI *moves.)* Not too much. Good. That's it. Right there. Good. *(*MIAMI *stops.)* Now when you tell this—when you start tellin' this I want you to get real animated. Almost like uh—almost like you were in a movie. Ya' know what I mean?

MIAMI: A movie?

HENRY: Yeah. Except more than a movie.

MIAMI: More?

HENRY: Much more. More like you were actually stepping back in time. Sort of re-living the experience of having been in Vegas. Ya' see what I mean?

MIAMI: I think so.

HENRY: I don't want you to just tell me some dumb story about some vague memory. I want to feel like I'm actually there.

MIAMI: Okay.

HENRY: If I don't actually get the feeling of it then there's no point in tellin' it. Am I right?

MIAMI: Right.

HENRY: Okay. Now just relax. Are you ready?

MIAMI: Ready.

HENRY: Good. You may begin.

MIAMI: Thanks. *(takes deep breath, starts to tell story)* Well-Uh-Actually I remember the day I got hired as a chorus girl.

HENRY: Tell about that.

MIAMI: I was in the hospital. I mean I'd just gotten out of the hospital from hepatitis. I was still yellow. And my friend. This friend I had then. Her name was Ellen. She picked me up and we drove to this Shell station. And we went into the rest room and she started slapping make-up on me. She put rouge all over my face to take the yellow out. And she got me this dress. And she got me all dressed up and everything. So then we drove to this casino.

HENRY: Wait a second! Wait a second! I'm not getting the feeling of this at all. I mean you've gotta' move around a lot more and make-believe you're actually there.

MIAMI: But I'm not there!

HENRY: I know you're not there. Just make-believe you're there.

MIAMI: But I can't make-believe I'm there when I'm not there.

HENRY: Just pretend. It's easy. You can pretend anything.

LUNA: *(to* MIAMI*)* Go ahead. You might as well.

HENRY: You've just got to get into it a lot more.

MIAMI: All right! Jesus, I didn't think I was coming here to do a fucking audition!

HENRY: Well, just do your best.

Pause. MIAMI *starts to tell the story again and tries to "act it out" for* HENRY.

MIAMI: So we drove up to the casino. And we went inside. And there was this guy. He was a great big guy.

HENRY: Wait! Start over.

MIAMI: What're you talking about!

HENRY: Start from the beginning again.

MIAMI: From the hospital?

HENRY: Right.

MIAMI *takes a deep breath and starts again, trying to "act it out."*

MIAMI: I was in California. In the hospital. I'd just gotten over having hepatitis. And this girl friend of mine picked me up and drove me to the airport.

HENRY: The airport? Last time it was the gas station.

MIAMI: *(crossing toward* HENRY *and* LUNA*)* I'm not doing this! Are you kidding?

HENRY: I'm sorry. I didn't mean to stop you but you did say the gas station the first time around.

MIAMI: I don't care what I said. I'm not doing it anymore! I'm gone. I'm tellin you, this guy is out of erasers as far as I'm concerned. I didn't come down here to get rousted! I don't care whose charge account it lands on. Who in the fuck does this sonofabitch think he is! Chargin around accusing me of double espionage! The guy's totally whacko! *(she whips up her coat from the platform)* I came down here for a little vacation not a goddamn brain bath!

LUNA: *(crossing down center)* I'll do it!

HENRY: Good! That's the spirit! That's exactly the kind of enthusiasm we need around here. That's what's been missing. *(to* MIAMI*)* You come and stay here and we'll watch her do it.

LUNA: *(to* HENRY*)* You want another Vegas story? Is that it?

HENRY: I don't want another Vegas story. I want the same Vegas story.

LUNA: But that's her story.

HENRY: What difference does it make? It's a good story. One story's as good as another. It's all in the way you tell it. That's what counts. That's what makes the difference.

LUNA: You want me to tell you her story?

HENRY: Why not?

LUNA: Because I don't know what her story is.

HENRY: Make it up. It's all the same.

LUNA: You want me to pretend that I'm her?

HENRY: Just take a plunge and stop pussy-footing around!

LUNA *starts "acting out" the story for* HENRY

LUNA: All right. Let's see. I'd just gotten out of the hospital and I was very yellow. Still very yellow. And a good friend of mine named Ellen picked me up and drove me to a Shell station.

HENRY: *(to* MIAMI*)* She remembers it better than you.

LUNA: *(continuing story)* First of all she washed off my face. And I remember her face while she was doing it. She looked like she felt sorry for me. Like she was taking pity on me. Then she started putting make-up on me. All kinds of make-up. Green eye shadow and rouge and lipstick. I looked like a different woman.

HENRY: *(to* MIAMI*)* Now we're getting somewhere. You see? You see what it takes?

LUNA: *(continuing)* Then she drove me out to the airport and put me on a plane for Montreal.

MIAMI: *(interrupting)* No, it wasn't Montreal. It was Vegas. First it was Vegas.

HENRY: *(to* MIAMI*)* Let her tell it the way she wants to tell it!

MIAMI: Look, it's my story! If she's gonna tell my story she's gotta' tell it right.

HENRY: *(to* LUNA*)* All right. Just change it to Vegas.

LUNA: *(checking with* MIAMI*)* It was Vegas first?

MIAMI: That's right. Vegas first. Then Montreal.

LUNA: *(continues story)* Okay. First it was Vegas. I went into this casino and there was this great big guy sitting on a tall red stool in the bar. I told him I'd come for the auditions. He sent me into a back room Introduced me to this ballet instructor who teaches me a few basic steps. Then they send me into another room where the guy who does the hiring is. And he look at my legs. All the usual stuff. Says, "Fine." And I'm on my way to Montreal.

HENRY: What about the airport?

LUNA: First I went to the airport and got on a plane and flew to Montreal.

HENRY: No, no, no!! It doesn't make sense! It's gotta' make some kind of sense! It's too confusing. First you're in Montreal then you're in Vegas. What the hell's goin' on here! *(HENRY suddenly gets alarmed)* Wait a second! Who are you people! *(MIAMI moves away from HENRY down toward LUNA, HENRY starts yelling off stage)* RAUL! RAUL! SOMEBODY'S BROKEN IN HERE! RAUL!

HENRY scrambles for the brass bell as he continues yelling for Raul. He enters and carries a World War I leather aviator's jacket, leather helmet, blue silk scarf and goggles over one arm. HENRY continues ringing the bell with his back to the platform, unaware of the activity behind him. Stops ringing the bell. RAUL holds out the jacket, helmet and goggles to HENRY. HENRY stares at them.

HENRY: *(to RAUL)* What the hell's that?

RAUL: It's the best I could come up with. Hard to find this stuff nowadays.

HENRY grabs the gear out of RAUL'S hands, moves back on his chair. HENRY glares at the two women then turns to RAUL.

HENRY: Did you invite these women in here?

RAUL: No sir.

HENRY: I want them out of here! Right now! I want them outa' here!

RAUL: Yes sir. *(to women)* Sorry, ladies.

LUNA: *(stepping twards HENRY)* Wait a second—

HENRY: *(violently, trembling with rage)* Out! Out! Out! Out! Out!

HENRY is gasping for breath and passes out. RAUL moves to him tries to calm him down, rubbing his shoulders.

HENRY: Who in the hell's making the decisions around here anyway!

RAUL: Only you sir.

HENRY: Only me?

RAUL: Yes sir.

HENRY: There's no one over my head somewhere? Somewhere lurking?

RAUL: Not a soul sir.

HENRY: How can you be sure of that, Raul? How can you be absolutely positive? These women didn't come on my invitation! That's impossible!

RAUL: It may have been an oversight, sir.

HENRY: An oversight! I can't afford an oversight! Not now.

RAUL: We won't let them out of the building without a thorough interrogation.

HENRY: Something's happening, Raul. Something's happening that I can't put my finger on.

RAUL: How do you mean, sir?

HENRY: I mean—the earth. Is the earth shaking? *(sudden panic)* Is that the earth shaking, Raul!

RAUL *presses firmly on* HENRY'S *shoulders*

RAUL: There's nothing shaking, sir.

HENRY: That sound! There's a sound! Down here the earth opens up sometimes. From time to time it swallows people. I've heard of that.

RAUL: It's all right, sir. There's no sound.

HENRY: Don't tell me there's no sound! Listen to that! Just listen.

RAUL *and* HENRY *listen. Silence.*

RAUL: There's nothing, sir.

HENRY *keeps listening. Long pause.*

HENRY: Is there someone watching me, Raul? Is that what it is?

RAUL: No one's watching you sir.

HENRY: Someone has to be watching me. I wouldn't feel this uneasy otherwise.

RAUL: Would you like some more plasma sir?

HENRY: Yes! Anything. Give it a mix. Give it a stir before you bring it in here.

RAUL: Yes sir.

RAUL *rushes off to get the blood. Women follow.* HENRY'S *left alone. He puts the blue scarf around his neck. He stares out at his palm trees. His eyes go from one palm to the other. He climbs off his chair and makes his way down to the stage right palm slowly, his arm reaching out in front of him. He talks to the palms.*

HENRY: *(as he walks toward palm)* Stop that shaking! Stop that! It's not necessary at a time like this. I'll tell you when to shake. You shake when I shake! The earth's not shaking so why should you.

HENRY *reaches the palm and grabs it with both hands as though to hold it still. He releases it and stands back. Looks at palm. Looks across at the other one.*

HENRY: That's better. Both of you. It's not my time yet. You'd agree to that. Both of you'd agree to that. I'm not completely at the end of my rope. There's other lives yet. More to come.

He darts a look at the stage left palm

HENRY: *(to palm)* Stop that shaking! *(he crosses quickly to the down left palm)* Stop it! There's no reason for it. No reason at all.

He grabs the stage left palm and steadies it the same as he did to the other one. When he's satisfied with the palm's stability he stands back and talks to it.

HENRY: *(to palm)* I have enough premonitions already without you creating more. The earth is firm. Temporarily firm. Once I take off then it can fall apart. You can shake all you want to then. *(pause.* HENRY *slowly tilts his head back and stares up at the sky.)* What's that moving? You feel that? There's something moving. Clouds. A fleet of planes. You hear that? You hear that sound? Thundering. Blue steel. They're trying to leave without me!

HENRY *suddenly panics. Moves center stage.*

HENRY: *(yelling)* Raul! They're evacuating the country without me! The President's leaving! The generals! They're trying to maroon me again! Abandon me to the elements! Raul! Where are my women! Get me my women before it's too late! Raul!

RAUL *comes rushing on with the intravenous rack and a fresh bottle of blood. He leaves the rack by the chair and moves down to* HENRY, *helping him back center stage to the chair.*

RAUL: *(helping* HENRY *walk)* You shouldn't get out of your chair sir.

HENRY: Where are my women! What's happened to my women!

RAUL: I brought you some fresh blood sir.

HENRY: We've got to get out of this place before the tidal wave. There is a tidal wave. You know that, don't you? Widespread devastation. Nevada's the only safe ground. Only Nevada. I have inside information. Tribal information.

RAUL: Yes sir.

RAUL *helps him back onto the chair, inserts the I.V. needle into* HENRY'S *arm and tapes it down.* HENRY *continues talking.*

HENRY: Las Vegas is on holy ground. Proof positive. I have definite verification on that.

RAUL: Just relax sir.

HENRY: Problem is the transit. Keeping it secret. Absolute secret. A black plane. Do we have the black plane?

RAUL: Yes sir.

HENRY: The jumbo?

RAUL: Yes sir.

HENRY: No markings of any kind?

RAUL: None sir.

HENRY: Radar spoiler?

RAUL: Yes sir.

HENRY: Zero to touchdown?

RAUL: That's right sir.

HENRY: So I'm to believe you've covered all the variables then?

RAUL: Who else can you believe sir?

HENRY: *(pause)* That's right. Who else. *(he picks up leather jacket and helmet)* This is my gear?

RAUL: Well it's just like what you used to wear.

HENRY: You mean this is stand-in gear? Dummy gear?

RAUL: Your original stuff exploded with that pilot over Nebraska.

HENRY: We don't talk about that!

RAUL: I'm sorry sir.

HENRY: I'm not supposed to hear about that!

RAUL: I forgot.

HENRY: Help me on with this stuff. You put it on me.

RAUL: Yes sir.

> RAUL *puts the goggles on over* HENRY'S *eyes, then the helmet. He helps* HENRY *on with the jacket, leaving the one sleeve loose over the intravenous arm.*

HENRY: Why am I shaking, Raul? Why am I constantly shaking?

RAUL: You're shaking less than you used to, sir.

HENRY: I'm not getting better am I? I'm getting worse.

RAUL: You'll be fine once we get across the border.

HENRY: Why should the border make any difference? I won't be safe until I hit Vegas. Sacred ground. Get my feet on sacred ground.

RAUL: You'll be fine, sir.

HENRY: You think I can still handle that plane? After all these years?

RAUL: It may be a little ambitious, sir.

HENRY: Ambitious? Of course it's ambitious! What's that got to do with it?

RAUL: I just meant physically sir.

HENRY: Physically? Physically. It's hard to believe I've still got a body left.

RAUL: The doctors say you're on the upswing.

HENRY: The doctors! Those Mexican goons?

RAUL: They're not Mexican sir.

HENRY: They're not American, either! This country's not fit for a man to get sick in. There oughta' be a law against falling ill in a foreign country. A man's got a right to die in his homeland.

RAUL: You're not dying yet sir.

HENRY: How can you live down here with monkeys crawling all over your food! Mosquitoes poisoning the water. We've gotta get outa' here!

RAUL: We will, sir.

HENRY: Those women are probably already contacting the papers. Blabbing about my whereabouts.

RAUL: They haven't left yet sir.

HENRY: Good. Keep them under surveillance. Constant surveillance. This is an evil time, Raul. Much worse than what I grew up in. Much, much worse. You've lost touch with things but I've still got the old inner radar to depend on. Still got the jump on the world at large.

RAUL: I've always respected your vision sir.

HENRY: My vision? That's right. My vision. I still see. Even in the dark, I still see. Do you want to know what I see, Raul? It's the same thing I saw in Texas when I was a boy. The same thing I've always seen. I saw myself. Alone. Standing in open country. Flat, barren. Wasted. As far as the eyes could take in. Enormous country. Primitive. Screaming with hostility toward men. Toward us. Toward me. As though men didn't belong there. As though men were a joke in the face of it. I heard rattlesnakes laughing. Coyotes. Cactus stabbing the blue air. Miles of heat and wind and red rock where nothing grew but the sand. And far off, invisible little men were huddled against it in cities. In tiny towns. In organizations. Protected. I saw the whole world of men as pathetic. Sad, demented little morons moving in circles. Always in the same circles. Always away from the truth. Getting smaller and smaller until they finally disappeared.

RAUL: I think your plane is ready sir. Is there any business you want to finish before we leave?

HENRY: Business? What business? My business is finished.

RAUL: Your will sir?

HENRY: My will? That's been decided. Everything goes to you, Raul. That's already been decided.

RAUL: But there's nothing on paper, sir.

HENRY: Paper's transient! Write it in the air. Air's the only thing that'll last forever.

RAUL: But the lawyers won't honor that sir.

HENRY: The lawyers! All the lawyers are good for is stealing you blind! They all work for the government. They're the ones who took my planes. Stole my planes right out from under me!

RAUL *suddenly pulls his pistol on* HENRY, *points it at his chest.* HENRY *stares at him. Pause.*

RAUL: *(quiet and firm)* I want something written on paper. Proof positive. I want it written in blood.

HENRY: What is this!

RAUL *moves into him suddenly and violently rips the intravenous drip from his arm.* HENRY *screams.* RAUL *holds the needle as blood spurts from it onto the floor. He holds the gun on* HENRY *with the other hand.*

RAUL: Get your papers out Henry. Under the bed.

HENRY: You can't do this to me! There's others over your head!

RAUL: There's no others, Henry. Just me.

HENRY: You're nothing but a bodyguard. A servant! What're you doing this for? I already told you it all goes to you. Don't you take me at my word?

RAUL: Nobody takes you at your word, Henry. Your word means nothing.

HENRY: I can have you annihilated in a second!

RAUL: By who? By what? You're nothing. You're not even a ghost. You don't even exist Henry. You've disappeared off the face of the earth. Nobody can trace you. We've made sure of that.

HENRY: I still have my executives! My trustees.

RAUL: Nobody. Nothing. It all stops at me.

HENRY: What've you done behind my back! What've you done to me!

RAUL: I've kept you alive for years and years. I've carried you on stretchers. I've cooked your spinach. I've bought you ice cream cones in the middle of the night. I've held you while you screamed. I've saved you from yourself, Henry. That's what I've done.

HENRY: I'm not signing anything! I'm not making anything final!

RAUL: You still don't believe it, do you?

HENRY: Believe what?

RAUL: That you're dying. You're finished. This is it, Henry.

HENRY: You can't kill me! You can't murder me!

RAUL: I can do anything I want, Henry. Anything. I can fabricate any story. Make up any lie. Have you disappear in London. Reappear in Brazil.

HENRY: That wasn't you! It was me! I was making the decisions! Only me!

RAUL: That's why it worked so beautifully, Henry. Because you believed it. Every suggestion we made, you believed it was your idea. That everything originated from you. The sole stockholder! The one and only Henry Malcolm Hackamore.

HENRY: I invented everything! My planes! My hotels!

RAUL: But not your life! Your life you left to us. To me. I shaped it for you. At first to suit your needs. And then to suit mine.

HENRY: You're a maniac!

RAUL: You can't make a move without me. Stand up! *(Pause.* HENRY *stares at him, still sitting on chair)* STAND UP! *(*HENRY *stands.* RAUL *smiles.)* That's right Henry. That's right. Now pull out your papers and put them on the chair.

HENRY *pauses, then does what he's told. He pulls out the box of manuscripts and sets it on the chair. He turns to* RAUL.

HENRY: I can't understand why you don't trust me. I can't understand it. I already told you I'd give you everything.

RAUL *moves to the box and starts pulling out the manuscripts. He hands the intravenous needle, still spurting blood, to Henry. Henry takes it.*

RAUL: *(handing needle)* Take this. *(thumbing through manuscripts)* This is where it counts, Henry. In these pages. This is where you give it away. All the secrets. All the treasures. This is what the world will believe. When they see it in black and white. *(he spreads manuscripts out on chair)* Now sign it. Every copy. Sign it with the needle. *(women enter)* I've arranged for a few witnesses. I hope you don't mind.

MIAMI *and* LUNA'S *laughter is heard off stage then the soft background sound of 40's dance music. The women come onto the upstage platform slowly, dancing cheek to cheek with the two doctors. The gangster follows behind, peering down from the platform at Henry. The music is* "You belong to me" *where the lyrics go* "Fly the ocean in a silver plane" *etc..* HENRY *watches the group on the platform then turns to* RAUL. *He still holds the needle with the blood dripping out of it.*

HENRY: *(to* RAUL*)* Will I still be able to fly?

RAUL: Anything you want, Henry. I've never refused you yet.

HENRY: I want to see Nevada again. Vegas. Vegas is the only place that makes sense. I can't die without seeing Vegas.

RAUL: You'll see it, Henry. Don't worry.

HENRY *starts signing the manuscripts with the dripping needle. The women look down at him over the shoulders of the doctors. The gangster watches* HENRY *closely.*

HENRY: I've never signed my life away before. There's nothing to it. No pain. Nothing.

RAUL: It should be a great relief.

HENRY: I don't feel a thing. It's as though it never happened. A whole life. Where's the proof, Raul? Where's the proof?

RAUL: Just sign. Just keep signing.

HENRY *continues signing the papers. The blood pours across the pages onto the floor.*

HENRY: I could've made the whole thing up. Any story I wanted. It's not even my blood, is it?

RAUL: By now it is. Your blood was used up a long time ago, Henry.

HENRY: *(starts to panic again)* It's not even my hand! My body! Whose body is this!

RAUL: *(moving in with gun)* Just sign, Henry. Just settle down and sign.

HENRY *continues signing papers.* RAUL *hovers around him. The platform action continues to the music.*

HENRY: *(signing)* In a second I see it. I see it now.

RAUL: What do you see?

HENRY: I see how I disappeared. It happened a long time ago. A long, long time ago.

RAUL: Where was it, Henry?

HENRY: Texas. That's the last time I lived on this earth. Texas. I disappeared in a dream. I dreamed myself into another shape. Another body. I made myself up.

RAUL: Keep signing, Henry.

HENRY: It happened in a second. In a flash. I was taken by the dream and all the time I thought I was taking it. It was a sudden seduction. Abrupt. Almost like rape. You could call it rape. I gave myself up. Sold it all down the river.

RAUL: It's too late to regret it now, Henry.

HENRY: But I still get to fly, don't I? You're still going to let me fly?

RAUL: Climb into the cockpit, Henry. Everything's waiting.

HENRY *starts climbing onto his chair to a standing position facing the audience as* RAUL *collects the manuscripts and piles them into the gangster's arms who's waiting on the platform. The blood drips from them onto the floor. The* WOMEN *keep dancing slowly with the doctors as the music continues underneath. As* HENRY *climbs the chair,* LUNA *starts singing the words of the song, softly, as she dances.*

LUNA: *(singing softly)*

"Fly the ocean in a silver plane
See the jungle when it's wet with rain
Just remember 'til you're home again
You belong to me
See the pyramids along the Nile."
(etc.)

LUNA'S *singing continues softly underneath* HENRY'S *voice.* RAUL *stays by* HENRY, *looking up at him, his pistol still drawn. The full moon in the background starts to slowly turn orange as the sky grows darker to the end of the act.*

HENRY: *(standing on the chair)* It's pitch black out here. Perfect. Perfect for escape. I think we did the right thing, RAUL. I can slip back in. No one will ever know the difference. They'll say I existed somewhere. A face. A name. No one will ever know for sure. You can take my place now. You can have it.

RAUL: You'll never escape Henry. You're standing on your bed. You'll never get out of here.

HENRY: *(slowly spreading his arms as though flying)* I've already left. I've gone. Come and gone. Just like that. Every seed I ever planted is growing. Look! *(he points far below him)* Look at it growing! Hotels! Movies! Airplanes! Oil! Las Vegas! Look at Las Vegas, Raul! It's glowing in the dark!

RAUL: You're nowhere, Henry!

HENRY: I'm everywhere! All at once I'm everywhere! I'm all over the country. I'm over Nevada!

RAUL *points the pistol at* HENRY *as* HENRY *soars on the chair with his arms spread. The sky gets darker. The moon grows red.* LUNA'S *singing fades out.*

HENRY: I'm high over the desert! Invisible. A ghost in the land. No voice. No sound. A phantom they'll never get rid of.

RAUL: You're dead Henry! You're dead! Lay down and die!

RAUL *fires the pistol at* HENRY. *The women and the doctors rush off stage. The music continues softly.* HENRY *doesn't die. He keeps flying.* RAUL *points the pistol at* HENRY'S *head.*

HENRY: I'm the demon they invented! Everything they ever aspired to. The nightmare of the nation! It's me, Raul! Only me!

RAUL *fires again.* HENRY *keeps raving and flying. He seems to get stronger with every blast of the pistol.* RAUL *goes down on his knees below* HENRY, *keeps firing at him but can't kill him.*

HENRY: I can move anywhere I want to now. Freer than life. Flying. My body's gone. You can't even see me now. Nothing can see me.

I'm dead to the world but I never been born.

I'm dead to the world but I never been born.

I'm dead to the world but I never been born.

I'm dead to the world but I never been born.

I'm dead to the world but I never been born.

I'm dead to the world but I never been born.

(repeat-fade with lights)

As HENRY *chants the lines, repeating the rhythm, his body slowly sways from side to side as his arms drop slowly to his sides. This should be a very slow, hypnotic movement as his voice fades in the chant.* RAUL *finally gives up firing the pistol and collapses forward on his knees in a gesture of supplication. The lights fade to black with the full moon remaining dark red behind the silhouette of* HENRY *standing on the chair. The voice of* HENRY *fades in the dark.*

SUICIDE IN B$^\flat$

A Mysterious Overture

Suicide was first produced at the Yale Repertory Theater in New Haven, Connecticut on October 15, 1976. It was directed by Walt Jones in association with Denise A. Gordon with the following cast:

Pianist: Lawrence Wolf
Pablo: Clifford David
Louis: Joe Grifasi
Petrone: William Hickey
Laureen: Alma Cuervo
Niles: Paul Schierhorn
Paulettea: Joyce Fideor
Music composed by: Lawrence Wolf

Slightly raked stage. A plain white muslin flat represents the upstage wall. It does not run the full width of the stage but leaves empty space on either side of it. It should be made obvious that it's a flat to the audience. There are no side walls. Dead center upstage, almost flush with the flat is a black upright piano. Not a grand piano. Downstage left is a blue stuffed arm chair with a brass floor lamp set to the upstage side of it. The lamp has a pale yellow shade with small green palm trees painted all around it in a circle. These are the only objects on stage. The floor of the stage is not painted but left bare. The entire set is visible to the audience as they come in. In the center of the floor, the outline of a man's body sprawled out in an awkward position of death is painted in white. The lights begin to dim very slowly. At their half way point, the PIANO PLAYER *rushes on from stage right, hiding his face from the audience with his coat, as though afraid to be photographed. He is wearing a shabby black suit. He sits quickly on the piano stool, back to audience and faces the piano. As the lights continue to dim, he raises both arms very slowly with the fingers of both hands interlaced until they are straight above his head. When he gets to the top of this stretch he cracks his knuckles loudly. The lights go to black. A loud gun shot is heard off stage, in the dark. Sound of a body falling hard to the floor. Lamp is switched on. Lights bank back up fast.* PIANO PLAYER *is still sitting at the bench with both arms still raised high, fingers together. Lights begin to slowly dim again. As they do,* PIANO PLAYER *lowers his arms slowly and sets them on the keys of the piano. He begins to play.* PABLO *and* LOUIS, *the two detectives, enter from right accompanied by the music.* LOUIS *is playing dead and being dragged across the floor by his heels by* PABLO. PABLO *is dressed in a long overcoat, baggy pants, shiny black shoes and a detectives hat.* LOUIS *wears striped pants, brown and white brogans, striped shirt and tie, black vest, black garters on his arms and a black detective's hat which he holds on his stomach while he's being dragged. The piano music continues as* PABLO *pulls him into center stage with some effort then drops both heels to the floor. Piano stops.* LOUIS *stays on the floor on his back.* PABLO *looks down at him.* PIANO PLAYER *just sits with back to audience. Lights stop at 1/2 level.*

PABLO: *(Catching his breath)* Trying to re-construct the imagination of it.

LOUIS: *(Still on his back)* What?

PABLO: The imagination. *(Between breaths)* The imagination of it. How we suppose it might have been. It's useless. All we come up with is "supposes."

LOUIS: Where's your brief case?

PABLO: *(suddenly hysterical, slapping his pockets as though he's lost something, going in circles)* Oh my God! What's happening to me!

LOUIS: You left it by the fire hydrant.

PABLO: Oh my God!

PABLO *rushes back off stage right.* LOUIS *slowly gets to his feet. He pauses a moment, standing there, looks down at the outline of the body on the floor. He pretends to be shot by a silent bullet and tries to fall into the shape of the outline. On the floor he checks out his position in relationship to the outline and adjusts his body accordingly.* PABLO *enters again from right with a big black brief case. He crosses straight to the arm chair down left, sits quickly, opens the brief case on his lap and worriedly checks through reams of typewritten papers.* LOUIS *stays on the floor.*

LOUIS: These positions remind me of hieroglyphs.

PABLO: It's lucky the whole thing wasn't ripped off. There it was, sitting there plain as a day. Just sitting on the cement.

LOUIS: The similarity between positions of death and the positions of birth are too awesome to be ignored.

PABLO: Will you get up off the floor and help me with this!

LOUIS: *(Sitting up)* What's to help? It's all there isn't it?

PABLO: How should I know! That's why I'm checking!

LOUIS: Well what if it wasn't all there? So what?

PABLO: Why are you so casual? Why are you always so goddamn casual!

LOUIS: *(Lays back down in position of outline)* The guy's dead, right?

PABLO: *(Still going through papers)* That's right. That's right. The guy's dead. Very brilliant.

LOUIS: This is all after the fact.

PABLO: Not if there's extenuating circumstances!

LOUIS: Don't use big words. It's embarrassing.

PABLO: I'm not afraid of my education! It serves me. It gives me a certain support. Even in the company of goons, it's a comfort. It gives me hope of a certain kind.

LOUIS: *(Still on floor)* What kind of hope?

PABLO: I'm not getting into this with you, Louis. Every time you sucker me into this I regret it. I'm not even going to start.

LOUIS *gets up off the floor quickly and crosses to the lamp beside*

PABLO. *He stares at the lamp shade and turns it in a circle with his hand.* PABLO *keeps pouring through the papers.*

LOUIS: Beautiful shade. Antique probably.

PABLO: *(Not looking up)* I doubt it on his salary.

LOUIS: *(Still turning shade)* Do composers get a salary?

PABLO: Commissions. Whatever. He didn't make much.

LOUIS: How come?

PABLO: Nobody bought it, that's how come! Nobody bought the music.
LOUIS *starts pulling the chain switch on the lamp, turning it off and on as he stares at the shade.* PABLO *keeps on with the papers.*

LOUIS: Nobody bought the music?

PABLO: That's right.

LOUIS: So he blew his brains out.

PABLO: That's a little over-simplified.

LOUIS: So he got depressed.

PABLO: We don't know that for sure.

LOUIS: Down in the dumps.

PABLO: We don't know.

LOUIS: That's no reason to blow your brains out. I mean, love is a better reason isn't it?

PABLO: I don't know! And stop switching that lamp on and off!
LOUIS *stops. Pause.*

PABLO: Why don't you go into the kitchen and make us a 'b.l.t.' while I go through these papers.

LOUIS: *(Moving back toward center)* It's not our kitchen.

PABLO: So what?

LOUIS: It's his kitchen.

PABLO: What're you superstitious or something?

LOUIS: I have my doubts.

PABLO: About what?

LOUIS: About being here so soon. I mean it wasn't that long ago he was dragged out of here.

PABLO: *(Throwing papers up in the air)* I can't find it anywhere in here! Our one piece of evidence and it's gone!

LOUIS: Don't get yer pants in a bunch. It'll turn up.

PABLO: Listen Louis! If you don't bottle this bullshit right here and now, I'm calling the Squad and asking them to send me a new man! I mean it Louis! I've had it!

LOUIS: You certainly have.

PABLO: I've had it up to here with your goddamn casual attitude! It's as though nothing matters. As though nothing's happened. We could be sitting in the Governor's mansion for all you give a shit.

LOUIS: I have a theory.

PABLO: There could be big stakes involved in this for us if you had eyeballs to see into the possibilities. If you thought for one second about the implications!

LOUIS: I have a theory.

PABLO: The ramifications. It's chocked full of juicy potential criminal action against some very big steam in some very high places and you can't even see beyond your own nose.

LOUIS: I have a theory. Do you wanna hear it?

PABLO: *(Pausing, catches his breath)* What theory?

PIANO PLAYER *begins to play, accompanying* LOUIS *as he speaks.*
PABLO *keeps going through the papers, half listening to* LOUIS.

LOUIS: *(Piano behind)* A boy hears sound. He hears sound before he has a name. He hears gurgling, pounding under water. He hears an ocean of blood swimming around him. Through his veins. Through his mother. He breaks into the light of day. He's shocked that he has a voice. He finds his voice and screams. He hears it screaming as though coming down through ancient time. Like it belongs to another body. He hears it that way. He hears the crack of his own flesh. His own heart. His skin sliding on rubber mats. Squeaking. He hears his own bones growing. Stretching his skin in all directions. Bones moving out. Organs expanding. The sound of cells booming through his brain like tiny inter-galactic missiles. Atoms. Nuclear rushes of wind through his nose holes. Toe nails rubbing blankets in the dark. Books falling on pianos. Electricity humming even when the lights are off. Internal combustion engines. Turbo jets. Then one day he hears what they call music. He hears what they call "music" in the same way he hears what they call "noise." In the same stream. Music as an extension of sound. An organization. Another way of putting it. He's disappointed. He's disappointed and exhilerated at the same time. Exhilerated because he sees an opening. An adventure. A way inside. He sees that putting any two things together produces sound. Any two things. Striking, plucking, blowing, rubbing, dropping, kicking, kissing. Any two things. He has a revelation. Or rather, a revelation presents itself. Stabs at him. Enters into him and becomes part of his physiology. His physiognomy. His psychology. His paraphernalia. His make up. He puts it to use. He's driven toward it in a way most men consider dangerous and suicidal. His production is abundant. Non-stop. Endlessly winding through un-heard-of-before symphonies. Concertos beyond belief. He organizes Quintets. Soloists rush to him just to be in his presence. The best ones are rejected. He only takes on apprentices. He only plays night clubs although he could pack out the 'Garden' in a flash. He shakes the sidewalks with his compositions. Every city in the world is calling his name. He invents totally new chord progressions and scales. New names for notes that not even the Chinese have heard of. Instruments that he makes in the bathtub. His music is sweeping the country. And then one day he disappears. Just like that. He goes. Not dead. Just gone. No one can figure it. Rumors are spread that he's kidnapped. Abducted and taken to Sweden. Then it switches to murder. Talk of him being involved with particular ladies of particular gentlemen. Then his body is found. His body is found but his face is blown off. His fingerprints are tested and they check out completely. His one-of-a-kind fingerprints. The case is closed.

PABLO: *(Short pause, still looking through papers)* Is that it?

LOUIS: No.

PABLO: There's more?

LOUIS: Yes.

PABLO: Well what is it?

LOUIS: He's fooled them all.

PABLO: How do you mean?

LOUIS: He's just laying low.

PABLO: *(Crossing, begins to pace,* LOUIS *crosses to chair)* That doesn't make any sense at all! He's got nothing to lay low for.

LOUIS: Aha! We don't know that for sure. That's where the case gets interesting.

LOUIS *sits in chair and starts going through papers as* PABLO *paces back and forth.*

PABLO: He was at the top of the bill. Maybe not as high up as you depict but pretty goddamn high up there. Why disappear when things are going so good. It's crazy.

LOUIS: But Possible.

PABLO: It's a crazy theory! *(Sees* LOUIS *with papers)* Stay away from those papers!

PABLO *rushes over to* LOUIS *and grabs the papers out of his hands.*

PABLO: Just keep your hands off!

LOUIS: Look, I'm on this case too. This stuff's not confidential.

PABLO: Oh yeah! Not confidential, huh? Who the hell called me up in the middle of the goddamn night, worried sick, and wanted to know if these papers were under lock and key? Who do you suppose?

LOUIS: I haven't the faintest.

PABLO: The Governor! That's who, wise ass! The Governor! Not confidential my ass. They're Super-Confidential! They're so confidential, they're even classified. That's how confidential they are. Classified by a top flight agency. I'm not at liberty to say any more about it.

LOUIS: You've become a blithering idiot, Pablo. A total meatball. Those papers are as valuable as yesterday's *Daily News.* There's nothing in there but palilalia. Do you know what "Palilalia" is?

PABLO: I'm not talking.

LOUIS: Well "palilalia" is what you've got. "Palilalia" is what you've got right there in you hamburger hands. And that's all you've got.

PABLO: I know you've been trying to sabotage this project right from the start. Right from the very beginning. There's something in you that wants to destroy me.

LOUIS: You're a turkey Pablo. A total turkey.

PABLO: I don't see any possible way that we can work together. I just don't see how it's possible. It would be hard enough working with someone who's compassionate and sensitive and at least showed an interest in the case but you're totally negative.

LOUIS: Indifferent.

PABLO: That's worse than negative!

LOUIS: I'm trying to remain objective about this.

PABLO: Objective my ass! You're dead weight Louis! Dead weight!

LOUIS *stands suddenly, listening intently for a noise. No sound.*

LOUIS: What was that?

PABLO: What was what?

LOUIS: That.

They both listen for a second. Again nothing.

PABLO: Not only are you dead weight but you're a lunatic.

LOUIS: No, listen!

PABLO: I'm not going to listen! I'm through listening.

LOUIS: Like a woman screaming. A terrible screaming. Like a woman being tortured.

PABLO: It's your ears Louis! Your ears are telling you stories.

LOUIS: *(Crossing toward outline on floor)* I don't like the idea of having this outline of a dead man on the floor with us. It's primitive. There's something creepy about it.

PABLO: Don't touch it until the Squad gets here!

LOUIS: I'm not going to touch it.

PABLO: What is it with you anyway? Have you completely lost touch with your vocation?

LOUIS: I'm wasting away. At least half of me is wasting away.

PABLO: Pull yourself together.

LOUIS: You didn't hear a voice?

PABLO: Of course not.

LOUIS: Don't be so smug about it. You're totally ignorant of what's going on here. You're blundering around in here as though this was just another ordinary old homocide. You're blinded by your career.

PABLO: I'm not distorting the facts yet, if that's what you mean.

LOUIS: You don't have any facts!

PABLO: And you don't have any sense! *(Pause as they stare at each other)* Now let's get to work.

LOUIS: What now?

PABLO: A stabbing. We haven't tried a stabbing yet.

LOUIS: His face was blown off.

PABLO: There's no report from ballistics!

LOUIS: You don't need a report when someone's face is blown away.

PABLO: It could've been carved off. Now you stand over there where the body was found and I'll come at you with a butcher knife.

LOUIS: Have you got a butcher knife?

PABLO: I'll get a butcher knife. Now you just stand there and wait.

PABLO *exits up left.* LOUIS *stands center stage. Simultaneously with* PABLO'S *exit,* PETRONE *enters from stage right. He's tall and extremely skinny, wearing baggy pants, T-shirt and suspenders. He has an alto saxophone strapped to his neck. He bites down on the mouthpiece and mimes blowing it. No sound comes from the sax but a high shrill scream of a woman is heard off stage. It should be delivered like a musical note but definitely be a scream. It stays on one note for ten full seconds as* PETRONE *keeps blowing silently into the horn.* LOUIS *does not hear the scream. He just stands there. Suddenly* PABLO *rushes on very fast from stage left holding a butcher knife high above his head as though he's going to stab* LOUIS. *He stops just short of* LOUIS *with his arms still raised holding the knife. Scream stops.* PETRONE *takes his mouth off the sax.*

PABLO: I can't do it.

LOUIS: You're not supposed to do it. If you did it, I'd be dead.

PABLO *drops the knife to the floor and goes to the chair and collapses into it.* LOUIS *bends over and picks up the knife.* PETRONE *crosses into the center area.*

PETRONE: *(To* LOUIS*)* You seen Niles?

LOUIS: Niles? No. Why?

PETRONE: We were supposed to get together.

PABLO: *(Still in chair)* I can't get it up. I can't get it up for this. What's happening to me? I've waited a lifetime for a case like this. And now I can't get it up.

PETRONE: *(Crossing toward chair, to* PABLO*)* Do you mind if I sit in that chair? That's the chair I always sit in.

PABLO: Yes I do mind. I'm having a nervous breakdown as a matter of fact.

PETRONE: Well do you mind if I sit on your lap then? I've gotta sit down. My bones are snapping.

PABLO: *(To* LOUIS*)* Who is this guy? *(To* PETRONE*)* Sure! Sure, sit on my lap! What the hell! The whole case is going to pot anyway.

PETRONE *sits down on* PABLO'S *lap. He smiles at* LOUIS *who is still handling the knife.*

PETRONE: *(To* LOUIS*)* You guys are awful nice. You know that? Awful nice. I'm part of the scum of the earth. You know what I mean. Low DOGS. Lower in fact. It's a caste system. Don't you agree? Wouldn't you guys agree to that?

LOUIS: Sure.

PETRONE: Same as they got in India. Wouldn't you say? Same story over here. No different.

LOUIS: No different. That's for sure.

PETRONE: There's more disguises over here I guess. More ways of covering it up. But I have a theory that it's something we're born with. You know what I mean? I mean it seems like I'll never get out of it.

LOUIS: You're right. You won't.

PETRONE: You won't either.

LOUIS: I might. But you definitely won't.

PETRONE: You're right.

PABLO: Would you mind shifting a little bit?

PETRONE: *(Shifting his weight on* PABLO's *lap)* Oh sure. Sorry about the bones. This time of year they get particularly menacing. One time it got so bad they came right out at the elbows. Right straight out like two white fish.

LOUIS: You mean out of the skin?

PETRONE: Sure. Like two white fish. I almost blinded people in the day time. The sun bounced right off them like ivory. Right into people's faces. People bounced back, holding their eyes, screaming in pain. It was a great feeling of power it gave me. A great feeling. Like I possessed certain laser rays within my elbows and if anyone fucked with me I just pointed them in the right direction.

PABLO: Get off my lap please.

PETRONE: No.

LOUIS: *(After pause)* You were supposed to meet Niles here?

PETRONE: I am meeting him. That's what I'm here for. We're going to play.

LOUIS: He's dead.

PETRONE: No he's not.

LOUIS: Yes he is.

PETRONE: No he's not.

LOUIS: Yes he is.

PETRONE: No he's not.

LOUIS: *(After pause)* Get off my partner's lap please.

PETRONE: *(Laughing)* Your partner? This is your partner? Like Gabby Hayes? You remember Gabby Hayes?

LOUIS: Yes I do remember Gabby Hayes as a matter of fact.

PETRONE: What're you guys doin here anyway? This isn't your house.

PABLO: We probably have more of a right to be here than you do. In fact we're fully within our rights.

LOUIS: We're investigating a murder.

PABLO: A possible murder.

PETRONE: You're detectives?

LOUIS: That's right.

PETRONE: Like Dick Tracy! You remember Dick Tracy?

LOUIS: *(After pause, fondling knife)* If you don't get off my parner's lap *(Pause)* I don't know what I'm going to do.

PETRONE: I remember Dick Tracy. *(He gets off* PABLO'S *lap and crosses up stage)* I remember all about him. Two-way wrist radio. His yellow hat. His black Mercury.

LOUIS: Are you part of Nile's band?

PETRONE *turns to* LOUIS *and stares at him. He puts the saxophone to his mouth and starts to finger the keys. No sound from the sax except the rhythmic tapping of the keys. He keeps this up.* LOUIS *crosses over to* PABLO.

LOUIS: *(Confidentially to* PABLO*)* Are you all right?

PABLO: Don't be ridiculous.

LOUIS: *(Under his breath)* We've got to get out of here. This is worse than I expected.

PABLO: Don't panic. It could be our big break. I'll try to have a talk with him.

PABLO *gets up and crosses to* PETRONE *who continues fingering the sax.*

LOUIS: It's too dangerous Pablo! You don't know what you're getting into.

PABLO: *(To* PETRONE*)* You've known Niles for some time I take it?

PETRONE *keeps blowing silently into sax and fingering keys.*

LOUIS: He's burned out, Pablo. You won't get anywhere with him. I say we go back to headquarters and file a report.

PABLO: Do you know if he had any girl friends?

PETRONE *stops 'playing' sax for a second and looks hard at* PABLO.

PABLO: Any lady friends that we might be able to have a talk with?

PETRONE *puts the sax back in his mouth and 'plays' silently again.*

LOUIS: Leave him alone and let's get out of here!

PABLO: *(To* PETRONE*)* Any rackets?

LOUIS *suddenly puts the butcher knife up to his own neck as though about to kill himself.* PABLO *and* PETRONE *pay no attention.*

PABLO: *(To* PETRONE*)* Was he involved in any side activities? Poppy seeds Parimutuels? O.T.B.? Anything like that?

LOUIS *starts to struggle with one hand against the hand that's holding the knife against his neck.* PABLO *and* PETRONE *continue without noticing.*

PABLO: It could be important. You see, I have a strong inclination that he didn't kill himself. I have the feeling he was under the influence of macabre overtones. A victim of odious events that spiraled toward his eventual downfall.

PIANO PLAYER *breaks in here, strong forceful bass line,* PETRONE *keeps playing silently.* LOUIS *struggles more desperately with the knife hand moving all over the stage,* PABLO *keeps talking.*

PABLO: A victim of circumstances beyond his control. He got in over his head. He bought off more than he could chew. He began dallying with power figures. He was sinking in a sea of confusion. His music was driving him mad. His improvisations were lasting for days on end. He had to be dragged from his piano and strapped to his bed. Fed intravenously to keep him from starving. He forgot how to speak and only uttered noises of varying pitch. His gestures were all in slow motion as the shock of fast movement was too loud for his ears. He began to feel certain that he was possessed. Not as if by magic but by his own gift. His own voracious hunger for sound became like a demon. Another body within him that lashed out without warning. That took hold of him and swept him away. Each time with more and more violence until his weaker side began to collapse. He was desperate for some kind of help so he turned to religion. Superstition. Cultism. There were plenty of self-proclaimed 'healers' ready to take him on. Waiting like hyenas in the wings. He gave himself over to them willingly. Anything that promised to deliver him from this nightmare. He followed their every demand. His music was written to their specifications. His money was put in their hands. His thoughts were geared to their dogma. And his demon began to be tamed. It changed its attitude completely and started to toe the line. His music turned into boring melodics. Slowly he noticed the change. He liked the new feeling of freedom. He thanked his masters and told them that now that the demon had left him he would go off on his own again. But they told him he couldn't. That he was still in danger. That as long as he was within their power he'd be all right. He'd be safe. He argued with them for weeks on end. His mind would go back and forth between submission and rebellion. His music was turning to pablum. Finally he decided to leave them completely. And that's when they killed him.

Piano stops. PETRONE *stops.* LOUIS *falls to the floor, exhausted from the struggle. The knife falls from his hand.*

LOUIS: *(Breathing heavily, on floor)* Pablo, we've got to get out of here!

PABLO: *(To* LOUIS *crossing back to chair and papers)* Get up off the floor. We're through with simulating events now. Now we've got some real evidence.

PETRONE: *(To* PABLO*)* That's not the way it happened at all. You guys are really off the deep end.

PABLO: Ah! Then you admit something did happen! That's more than you were admitting before.

LOUIS: There's no evidence Pablo!

PETRONE: You guys better get outa' here before Niles comes back.

PABLO: Where's he gone to?

PETRONE: He went out to get some toasted English muffins. That's the only thing he eats when he's working.

PABLO: Where did he go to get the toasted English muffins?

PETRONE: Hey, lighten up buster. This is my day off.

PABLO: *(Suddenly intent crossing slowly toward* PETRONE*)* What do you know about improvisation?

PETRONE: You talkin to me?

LOUIS: *(Still on floor)* Pablo, will you leave him alone!

PABLO: *(To* PETRONE*)* Yes. You claim to be one of Niles' musicians. I haven't heard a sound come out of your horn yet.

PETRONE: You haven't?

PABLO: No, I haven't.

PETRONE: Well, it takes a while to attune your ears to the frequency we're playing in. It's extremely high. Dogs can't even hear it. That's why Niles has trouble selling it.

PABLO: I see.

PETRONE: It's also an attempt at visual music. You'll have to wait for Niles to come so he can explain it to you. I know how to play it but I can't explain it.

PABLO: I can't wait for Niles.

LOUIS *starts struggling with his hand again as it tries to reach for the knife. He grabs it with the other hand pulls it back. The hand reaches out again for the knife, etc..*

PETRONE: You guys are very pushy, you know that? I'm not even used to talking and you're trying to force me into explanations.

PABLO: What do you know about improvisation?

PETRONE: Will you get off that kick! That's not something to mess around with. That's private!

PABLO: How does it relate to breaking with tradition! To breaking off with the past! To throwing the diligent efforts of our fore-fathers and their fore-fathers before them to the winds! To turning the classics to garbage before our very eyes! To distorting the very foundations of our cherished values! *(Piano breaks in with loud atonal chords at random intervals)* To making mince-meat out of brilliance! To rubbing up against the very grain of sanity and driving us all to complete and utter destruction! To changing the shape of American morality! That's where it's at! That's where it's at isn't it! You've snuck up on us through the back door. You're not strong enough to take us over by direct political action so you've chosen to drive us all crazy. Then, when we're all completely within your control, you'll take us over. That's it isn't it? You're getting back at us after all these years. I wasn't born yesterday you know! I know a thing or two! I know when I'm being bushwhacked!

(Piano stops.)

LOUIS: *(From floor, reaching for knife.)* Pablo! Could you reach me the knife?

LAUREEN *enters from stage right dressed in a bathrobe and wheeling an acoustic double bass fiddle in front of her. The bass is contained in a canvas case. As soon as she enters she screams on a high note and continues the scream until she's crossed to center stage. She stops center stage and ends the scream. She unzips the canvas case, takes out a bow and starts bowing the bass on random notes. It makes no difference if she knows how to play.* PABLO *circles around her, taking note of the new development.* PETRONE *crosses down to the chair and sits in it. He starts going through* PABLO's *papers.* LOUIS *keeps reaching for the knife on the floor. There is a while that passes with no talk.*

PETRONE: *(To* PABLO, *in chair as he browses through papers.)* There was a time when I felt like that myself. As though a particular group was at the heart of it. As though secret organizations were constantly plotting against me. Not just against me but against all members of my particular caste. The Low Dogs. Gang warfare on an international scale. It got so that I felt they were personally responsible for a bad count of smack.

LAUREEN: *(As she bows the bass, to* PABLO.*)* Your partner is reaching for the knife.

PABLO: *(As he circles around her.)* Yes, I know.

LAUREEN: *(To* PABLO*)* You should tell him that everything's all right. There's no need for that kind of stuff now. He's extending himself needlessly.

PABLO: *(Still circling* LAUREEN *as she plays.)* How long have you known Niles?

LAUREEN: We've gone through that particular era. Something new is called for now. There's no need for remorse. He's defeating the purpose.

PABLO: Just answer the question!

LAUREEN: *(Still playing)* You should tell him not to jump to conclusions. There's no organization strong enough to make you crumble. There's no system stronger than a single man. He should just stand up and forget about the whole thing. What's he killing himself for anyway? An audience? There isn't any audience. Tell him there isn't any audience. Tell him that.

PABLO: HOW LONG HAVE YOU KNOWN NILES! ANSWER THE QUESTION!

(She stops playing and looks at PABLO.*)*

LAUREEN: *(To* PABLO*)* Long enough. *(She looks at* LOUIS.*)* Will you get up off the floor please? It's distracting.

LOUIS *stops reaching for the knife. He looks at her.*

LOUIS: *(To* LAUREEN, *from floor.)* Isn't the nation broken in half?

LAUREEN: No way of telling.

LOUIS: Aren't we leaderless? Jobless? Destitute? Forlorn?

LAUREEN: Just get up.

LOUIS: Not until I get some guarantees!

PETRONE: *(From chair, with papers.)* Let him kill himself. Who gives a fuck.

PABLO *rushes over to* PETRONE *and grabs the papers out of his hands.*

PABLO: *(To* PETRONE*)* Stay away from those papers!

LAUREEN: *(To* LOUIS*)* Personally, it doesn't matter to me one way or the other if you kill yourself. It just seems pointless.

LAUREEN *goes back to bowing the bass,* LOUIS *stays on floor,* PABLO *goes through his papers,* PETRONE *sits in chair.*

LOUIS: *(To* LAUREEN*)* To you it would seem pointless! You've got a particular calling. You've got an obsession. The whole structure can collapse around you and you wouldn't mind. You'd just sit there fiddling away like Nero or something. *(Suddenly hysterical, throwing himself around on the floor.)* IT'S DIFFERENT WITH ME! I'M DOWN HERE ON THE GROUND! I'M WAY DOWN HERE! YOU CAN'T EVEN SEE ME I'M SO LOW!

PETRONE: *(To* PABLO*)* I'm lower than him.

LAUREEN: *(casually to* LOUIS *as she plays.)* Pick yourself up.

LOUIS: Stop saying that to me! I'm a detective! I should be ordering you around! I should be the strong one!

LAUREEN: But you're not.

LOUIS: Pablo, call her off! She's trying to destroy my opinions!

PABLO: *(Calmly to* LAUREEN *and* PETRONE*.)* It's time for you people to leave now. You've been very helpful. We'll call you if we need any further information.

PETRONE: *(To himself)* We need another martyr like a hole in the head.

LOUIS: I'M NO MARTYR! I'M A DETECTIVE!

PABLO: Louis, get up.

LAUREEN: *(Still playing)* This music has no room for politics. It answers to nobody. It plays by itself even when we're not playing it. Even when we're not there to listen. It has no boss. Even when the Boss is dead it keeps playing.

PABLO: *(Suddenly lunging toward* LAUREEN*)* Was Niles the boss? Was that it?

LAUREEN: *(Still playing)* Even when idiots surround it on all sides.
PETRONE *stands suddenly.* LAUREEN *stops playing.*

PETRONE: *(To* PABLO*)* I'll tell you the whole story. You wanna' hear it? I'll tell you the whole thing. It's no secret.

PABLO: *(Rushing to* LOUIS*)* Louis, get up! He's going to spill the beans. Get up! Get up!

LOUIS: Right now?

PABLO: Get up! Come on. We've finally forced their hand.
PABLO *helps* LOUIS *to his feet and takes him over to the arm chair. He sets* LOUIS *down in the arm chair and then sits on his lap.* PETRONE *moves center stage.* PIANO PLAYER *begins to play behind* PETRONE. LAUREEN *accompanies on the bass.*

PETRONE: The story of Niles from the top:

LOUIS: Is he going to tell us a story?

PABLO: *(Sitting on* LOUIS' *lap)* He's going to tell us the whole story.

LOUIS: I could've easily killed myself, you know.

PABLO: It's all right now. It's going to be all right. We've got them just where we want them. They're playing right into our hands.

PETRONE: *(To* LOUIS *and* PABLO*)* Niles was a big man. A huge man in fact. The kind of man you'd take to be a brakeman before anything else.

NILES *enters from up right with a flashlight. He's accompanied by* PAULLETTE, *a skinny young girl in a skimpy dress with a blanket over her shoulders. She carries a large suitcase.* NILES *is very big, dressed in a crumpled black suit, dark glasses and a black hat. They both sneak on tip-toes very slowly toward center stage. The others do not relate to them. Piano accompanies them.* PETRONE *narrates but does not direct anything to* NILES *and* PAULLETTE.

NILES: *(Half whisper)* You sure it's not too soon Paulette? They could be waiting around in there.

PAULLETTE: No, it's perfect. If you waited any longer you'd give them time to figure it out.

NILES: Don't the streets smell funny?

PAULLETTE: They smell wet.

PETRONE: *(To* LOUIS *and* PABLO*)* His hands were so huge they could stretch two octaves in a single stroke. Not even Art Tatum could boast such hands. Not even Joe "Fingers" Carr. The kind of hands that looked capable of breaking a young calf in half.

NILES *and* PAULLETTE *approach the center playing area and stop at the edge of it.*

NILES: *(whispering)* You better take a look inside, just to make sure.

PAULLETTE *goes up on her tip-toes as though looking through a window.*

NILES: See anything?

PAULLETTE: Nothing. Just an outline of your body on the floor.

NILES: Nothing else?

PAULLETTE: Nope.

NILES *and* PAULLETTE *sneak their way into the center stage area, amongst the other players who ignore them.* PETRONE *keeps narrating. Piano keeps playing.* LAUREEN *accompanies on bass.* LOUIS *and* PABLO *are spellbound watching* PETRONE *tell the story.*

PETRONE: As a child he was held in contempt by the other children because of his giant proportions. The kids called him "Brontosaurus Morris" and other nasty things. He was totally awkward as an adolescent and couldn't even speak a full sentence until the age of eighteen.

Suddenly the music stops, the stage lights go black. Only NILE'S *flashlight is seen. Then a pale follow spot comes on, illuminating* NILES *and* PAULLETTE. *The others stay motionless.*

NILES: What happened?

PAULLETTE: *(In a heavy whisper)* We're inside. It's all right. We're inside now.

NILES: No one's here?

PAULLETTE: Just us.

NILES: Did you hear someone screaming?

PAULLETTE: No Niles. It's o.k. now.

NILES: I just want to do it and get out of here.

PAULLETTE: We don't have to rush. We got plenty of time.

NILES: I feel like I shouldn't have come back. I already escaped. How come I came back?

PAULLETTE: *(Setting suitcase down center on the ground and opening it.)* We just gotta' do this one thing and then we'll be gone.

PAULLETTE *starts taking different pieces of clothing and masks out of the suitcase as* NILES *moves around the stage with the flashlight, shining it in different areas. Once in a while the flashlight crosses somebody's face but he doesn't linger on it. The stage lights stay dark. Just the flashlight and the follow spots.*

NILES: It's not so easy to leave a life. It's not the easiest thing in the world. I can still smell myself in this place. It feels like I never left.

PAULLETTE: It'll be different.

NILES: When?

PAULLETTE: Just take it easy.

NILES: *(Shining flashlight on outline on floor.)* Why do they still have this outline of my body on the floor? Maybe they're not convinced.

PAULLETTE: Stop worrying. They're convinced all right.

NILES: They've gone through all my papers! Look at my papers all over the place!

PAULLETTE: Go make yourself some coffee or something.

NILES: I just had a nightmare. I just had a nightmare while I was standing here.

PAULLETTE: What?

NILES: What if it turns out to be harder playing dead than it was playing alive?

PAULLETTE: That's not the way it works. You've got to give yourself time to settle into this thing, Niles. I'll explain the whole thing to you.

NILES: How come I'm trusting you? How come? All of a sudden I'm wondering that. I never questioned that before.

PAULLETTE: You know why.

NILES: I know you're not one of those big city models. I know that much. I know you're not hooked up to the politicians. The gangsters. The rackets. Dope syndicates. Numbers. Private Foundations. Federal Granting Organizations. C.I.A. Code Scanning. I know that much. I checked all that out. You're clean on that score.

PAULLETTE: O.K.

NILES: What I haven't checked out is the more insidious groups. The Mind Benders. The Chromatic Persuaders. The Psychic Transfusions. The Cult Mongers. All forms of ritualistic terrorism. That area is completely in the dark!

PAULLETTE: Don't shout.

NILES: *(Suddenly screaming)* THERE'S VOICES COMING AT ME!
PAULLETTE *jumps up and goes to him.*

PAULLETTE: Niles, quiet down! If they catch you here now, it's all over.

NILES: *(Screaming)* THERE'S VOICES FROM ALL SIDES!

PAULLETTE: There's nothing here now. You've shot yourself in the head and it's all over.

NILES: IT'S NOT! IT'S NOT OVER!

LAUREEN *lets out her shrill high scream again. Stage lights stay dark through this. Just follow spot. Piano comes in strong. Sax is heard live here, high wailing sounds.* LAUREEN *bows the bass in sharp rasping sounds.* NILES *moves frantically around stage to get away from the sound.* PAULLETTE *tries to calm him down. This lasts a short time and ends with a gun shot off stage and sound of body falling. Music stops. The lamp comes on, illuminating the shade.* NILES *stands and stares at it. Pause.*

NILES: *(Suddenly cooled out)* Do you know why I bought that lamp shade?

PAULLETTE: Why?

NILES: Because I was born on an island. I wasn't born in America you know. I was born way far away. I was imported. I lived in a tin house with a corrugated roof that sounded like Balinese cymbals when it rained. It rained tropical rains there. The kind that sound like they'll never end. And you'll be washed away. And you'll all be washed away. And at night the laundry flaps. The sheets snap like wet whips. They're all tied down by ropes so the Japanese don't steal them. And your mother has a .45 Automatic Colt Revolver with an extra clip in her pocket book just in case. And she takes you to the movies in an Army Jeep. Right through the monsoons in a Jeep to the Drive-In movies to watch *Song of the South*. *(Sings)* "Mr. Bluebird on my shoulder. It's the truth. It's actual. Everything is satisfactual. Zippety doo-da. Zippety ay. My oh, my oh what a wonderful day." *(Back to talk)* And the rain is pouring down in a sheet of green jungle water. Right over the movie screen. Like watching a movie through a waterfall. Right over the windscreen of the Jeep. And Mom has the .45 sitting right there loaded on her lap in case any Gooks stick their heads in the window. She'd blow their heads right off. Blow them right back out into the rain again.

PAULLETTE: That's why you got the lamp?

NILES: That's why I got the shade. I already had the lamp.

PAULLETTE: You wanna' lie down for a while?

NILES: No, I want to listen.

PAULLETTE: To what?

NILES: Whatever there is.

PAULLETTE: You want me to leave you alone for a while?

NILES: Doesn't matter. *(Continuing)* I got on a boat then. A tin boat with big holes in the deck that showed the ocean way down below. Sharks flashing by beer cans. Coral reefs. Island kids diving for American money. Silver dollars sinking to the deep blue seas.

PAULLETTE: Niles, you gotta get your head together now. You have to be clear about what your doing. No fuzziness.

NILES: I know, I know. That's important. It's a good thing you stopped me. I was about to go off the deep end again.

PAULLETTE: *(Moving toward suitcase)* Now come over here and try some of these things on.

NILES *moves to suitcase with* PAULLETTE. *The stage lights come back up as* NILES *starts taking off his clothes, one piece at a time and putting on pieces of a costume that* PAULLETTE *hands him from the suitcase. The costume is a kid's cowboy outfit. This change of costumes should be slow and deliberate as the focus switches to the others in the scene.*

LAUREEN: *(To* PABLO*)* Petrone shouldn't be telling you anything actually.

PABLO: *(Still sitting on* LOUIS' *lap)* How come? We're entitled to some information. We've been working for weeks on this case.

LOUIS: Could you move a little, Pablo? My knees are going to sleep.

PETRONE: *(To* PABLO*)* You know how Raymond Chandler worked? He always started out knowing who the killer was first and then spent the rest of the time covering it up. He always worked backwards. That's how you guys should do it.

PABLO: Just keep telling the story or I'm taking you all down to headquarters!

LAUREEN: This is headquarters.

PABLO: Don't get smart with me sister!

PETRONE: *(Moving slowly toward Pablo)* What exactly do you guys know anyway? Do you guys know anything?

PABLO: We know plenty.

PETRONE: Do you know anything about the nature of a nation?

PABLO: Don't try to dance around me with half-baked intellectual notions mister! I've been to school too!

LOUIS: Let him talk, Pablo. He's smarter than you.

PABLO: He's not smarter than me! He comes on like he's smarter but he's not. I've got a Master's Degree!

PETRONE: Small nations. Nations within nations.

LAUREEN: Don't give them too much rope Petrone.

PETRONE: *(To PABLO)* What's a musician to you?

PABLO: You're trying to confuse the issue but what you're not counting on is our single-mindedness. My single-mindedness. All this stuff doesn't matter. All this periphery. Extra frills. I'm here to discover what's at the heart of it. That's all that matters to me. The investigation.

PETRONE: What's a guy doing up there in front of dozens of people blowing his brains out on a horn for? What's he doing it for?

PABLO: How should I know! That's not my job to know that!

LOUIS: Pablo, get up!

PABLO: *(To LOUIS)* No.

LOUIS: *(Suddenly hysterical)* GET UP! I'M GOING CRAZY UNDER HERE! GET OFF ME!

LOUIS *throws* PABLO *off him.* PABLO *lands on the floor by the outline.* LOUIS *stands.*

LOUIS: I gotta' get out of here, Pablo! Something's not right! We've gotten ourselves into deep water here! Can't you feel it? Everything's crazy! I've got to get my bearings back. It feels like we're involved in something we'd be better off not knowing about. I never wanted to kill myself before. I've always had a good relationship with myself. A solid footing. I feel like I've slid into somebody else's head here or something. I'm used to Tommy Dorsey, the Mills Brothers,

Benny Goodman. All this free-form stuff is disturbing to my inner depths. It leaves me feeling nauseous. Like I'm going to throw everything up. Everything that's ever come into me. *(Starts moving frantically around stage, others stay still)* I'm a Republican by nature! That's what I am. I'm not ashamed of that! Eisenhower was my main man! We went through the war together. The Real War in the Real World! Why do I have to go through everything again! I'M NOT GUILTY! Am I guilty, Pablo? Answer me that!

PABLO: *(From floor)* You're not guilty.

LOUIS: Of course not! Of course I'm not! These dues belong to somebody else. Somebody else has to pay for this. IT'S NOT MY FAULT! I can't help it if things are in a state. I had to go to night school in my spare time to earn my diploma. The war took my time away. Took all my time away. I have shrapnel scars on the back of my neck. Pieces of hand grenade still embedded in my knees. I'm entitled to a little dance music! A nice waltz now and then. Three quarter time!

PABLO: *(Still on floor)* Louis, don't go crazy. The Squad needs you. You're one of our best men.

LAUREEN: *(To LOUIS)* You could always kill yourself.

LOUIS: You'd like that wouldn't you? It would be a mark of your success. There was a time when death was looked upon as a defeat!

PETRONE: When was that?

LOUIS: You're all so twisted around that you even have sane people thinking they're crazy. You've driven me and my partner to utter distraction! Look at my partner on the floor there! Once he was a proud man. He walked erect like the rest of us. Now he's groveling around on the floor!

LAUREEN: Pick him up.

LOUIS: You've made us lose track of our mission. We came here to get to the bottom of an evil act. We're working for the right side!

PETRONE: Suicide?

LOUIS: Murder in the first degree! A man doesn't blow his face off if he wants to kill himself. His face is something personal right up to the end. Even if he shot himself in the mouth it wouldn't blow his whole face off.

PETRONE: He wanted to remain mysterious. Anonymous.

LOUIS: You want him to remain mysterious! It's you that's hiding him from us.

LAUREEN: He's right here now.

LOUIS: I know he is. You've got him tucked away somewhere and we're going to drag him out!

PABLO: *(From floor)* Louis, maybe we bit off more than we can chew. I'm even starting to hear voices now.

LAUREEN: *(Listening. Starts to play bass softly)* Listen to that. He's doing away with dominant sevenths.

PABLO: *(Ear to floor, rubbing the outline softly with his hand.)* Listen, Louis! Can you hear that? He's a virtuoso.

LOUIS: I don't hear a thing! Wind is blowing through my head.

PETRONE *starts to play sax silently.*

PABLO: *(From floor)* His body was right here. Right where I'm laying now.

LOUIS: I can't hear a thing.

PABLO: Listen. It's incredible. *(Puts his ear to the floor)*

Lights fade. Follow spots up on NILES *and* PAULLETTE. NILES *is all dressed in the cowboy outfit now.* PAULLETTE *turns him around in a circle, checking out the costume.* NILES *sings softly to himself as* PAULLETTE *keeps circling him, adjusting his costume.*

NILES: *(Singing softly)* Pecos Bill, Pecos Bill

Never died

And he never will

Oh, Pecos Bill

NILES: *(To* PAULLETTE, *talking)* I hate killing this one off first, Paullette. Can't we save this one til last?

PAULLETTE: They'll all be painful. Doesn't matter what order you do them in.

NILES: Then let's do this one last.

PAULLETTE: No.

NILES: But there's no guarantee I won't die along with him.

PAULLETTE: I guarantee it.

NILES: But you don't know how attached I am. I feel as though his skin is my skin.

PAULLETTE: He doesn't have any skin.

NILES: He has a heart doesn't he?

PAULLETTE: He's a parasite. He's sucking your blood.

NILES: But I used him all these years. It only seems fair that he'd take something out of me.

PAULLETTE: Wait a second. You're making it sound like this was all my idea. It was you who was going down the tubes, remember?

NILES: Yeah.

PAULLETTE: It was you who was looking for a way out. I'm only supplying the means.

NILES: But how can we be sure we're going about it in the right way. I mean it already back-fired once on us.

PAULLETTE: That was a mistake.

NILES: His whole face was blown off!

PAULLETTE: That was a mistake, all right!

NILES: I don't want my face blown off!

PAULLETTE: Your face isn't going to get blown off! Now turn around.

NILES: What?

PAULLETTE: Turn around. You're not supposed to see the weapon.

NILES: Oh, Jesus, now I'm really scared.

PAULLETTE: Just turn around.

NILES: I need some time. Just let me work through this a little first. Just a little while longer.

PAULLETTE: O.K., take as much time as you want. I don't care. You're only giving them more time to catch up to you.

NILES: You said they were convinced!

PAULLETTE: For a while. It doesn't mean we can stand still. We gotta keep moving.

NILES: Just let me walk through this a little.

PAULLETTE: Go ahead.

NILES *starts moving around.* PAULLETTE *stands watching him. Soft piano builds under this.*

NILES: I want to be clear about this. I was clear before but now I'm not so sure. I want to be sure. I want to get rid of all these ones so I can start over. Is that it? Is that what it was?

PAULLETTE: That's it.

NILES: All these ones have to go because they're crowding me up. They've gotten out of control. They've taken me over and there's no room left for me. They've stolen their way into my house when I wasn't looking.

PAULLETTE: You invited them.

NILES: I invited them but I forgot to ask them to go. If I don't get rid of them they'll strangle me or something.

PAULLETTE: Something.

NILES: They'll do me in.

PAULLETTE: They're doing you in right now.

NILES: Yes. I can feel that. But I'm not sure what I'll do without them either. I'm not sure that if I get rid of all of them that I won't be lonely.

PAULLETTE: You will be for a while.

NILES: I don't want to be lonely.

PAULLETTE: You'll get over it.

NILES: I will?

PAULLETTE: You'll go through it.

NILES: I'm afraid to be lonely. I can't stand the idea of it even. It's almost worse than dying.

PAULLETTE: It is dying.

NILES: That's the reason I invited them in to begin with. So I wouldn't have to feel that loneliness. That's the reason I invented music. It filled me up. I got so filled up that I couldn't go on. Now I gotta start over.

PAULLETTE: You gotta start from scratch.

NILES: But they showed me their music too. I borrowed from them. They showed me everything I know.

PAULLETTE: But now you can't get to anything new. It's always the same. You're repeating yourself.

NILES: I'm repeating myself, again and again. It's not even myself I'm repeating. I'm repeating them. Over and over. They talk to me all the time. *(Suddenly screaming)* THERE'S VOICES COMING AT ME!

PAULLETTE: Keep it together Niles.

NILES: *(Calmer)* You'd think in a nation this big there'd be someone to talk to.

PAULLETTE: You talk to yourself.

NILES: You talk to yourself and other people talk to themselves. I wonder where my voice is.

PAULLETTE: Inside. Coming out.

NILES: Where? I don't hear a thing. Now there's nothing inside. They've all gone home.

PAULLETTE: They've just shut up for a while.

NILES: They're hiding?

PAULLETTE: They're waiting to jump on you. Any second they can jump on you.

NILES: And that's why I gotta do them in?

PAULLETTE: One at a time.

NILES: They aren't gonna' like it.

PAULLETTE: They won't know what hit them.

NILES: They're gonna' start screaming when they find out.

PAULLETTE: Don't let them know.

NILES: I feel like a traitor.

PAULLETTE: Turn around.

NILES: Not yet. I want to know this one first before he goes.

PAULLETTE: You already know him.

NILES: Not well enough. Is he King of the Cowboys or something? Does he make his women walk in ditches because he's so short? Does he wear elevator cowboy boots? What's so terrible about him?

PAULLETTE: Nothing.

NILES: What have I got against him?

PAULLETTE: Nothing.

NILES: Then why does he have to go?

PAULLETTE: He's burning your time.

NILES: He's a hero, Paullette! He discovered a whole way of life. He ate rattlesnakes for breakfast. Chicago wouldn't even exist if it wasn't for him. He drove cattle right to Chicago's front door. Towns sprang up wherever he stopped to wet his whistle. Crime flourished all around him. The law was a joke to him. State lines. He sang songs to the Milky Way.

PAULLETTE: Turn him around, Niles.

NILES: You can't kill a hero!

Piano building through this.

PAULLETTE: He's no hero! He's a weasel! He's a punk psychopath built into a big deal by crummy New England rags.

NILES: He's a myth!

PAULLETTE: So are you!

NILES: You can't kill a myth!

PAULLETTE: Turn him around Niles! Show me his back side.

NILES: He doesn't want to die!

PAULLETTE: Do you?

NILES: YES!! I mean no! NO!

PAULLETTE: Any way you want it.

NILES: *(After pause, staring at* PAULLETTE*)* All right. But do it easy. NILES *turns his back to her. Piano builds.* PAULLETTE *goes to suitcase and pulls out a bow and arrow.* NILES *speaks with his back to her as she loads the arrow in the bow very slowly.*

NILES: *(To himself)* It's a bright day. The kind of day you'd never expect to die in. He's got one foot up on the brass rail. The worn elbows of his rawhide jacket are digging into the mahogany bar. The bartender used to be his barber when he was a kid. The dirt streets outside are full of life. Girls of every color are doing their afternoon shopping. Newspapers are printing the news.

PAULLETTE *aims the bow very slowly and trains it on* NILE'S *back. She pulls the arrow back inch by inch as he keeps talking.*

NILES: Farriers are hammering iron. Dogs are pissing on horses' legs. Scaffolds are being constructed. He sees the nation being built in every small activity. Everything looks like progress to him. Nothing looks like it could ever die. He doesn't see it coming. He never even knew what hit him. It was over in a flash.

PAULLETTE *lets the arrow go. It strikes him dead center in the back.* LOUIS *screams in the dark as the second the arrow strikes* NILES. NILES *stays standing with the arrow stuck in him. He makes no reaction. Follow spots out. Stage lights up.* NILES *starts taking off his cowboy outfit and* PAULLETTE *helps him on with another costume from the suitcase. Focus switches to others on stage.* LOUIS *is staggering around with an arrow stuck in his back, moaning and trying to pull it out.* PABLO *jumps up from the floor and starts searching the stage for possible attacker.*

LOUIS: *(Moving all over, trying to reach the arrow in his back)* I knew he was around! I knew it! We should've left someone on the door, Pablo!

PABLO: Don't anyone move!

PETRONE: We aren't going nowhere.

PABLO: Don't anyone touch anything! Don't anyone even breathe! We've got a psychopath on our hands!

LAUREEN: Aren't you guys going overboard a little with this whole thing? I mean, Christ, the poor guy's dead. Leave him lay.

LOUIS: He's not dead! He just shot me in the back! Look! I've been shot!

LAUREEN: It's just an arrow. Pull it out.

LOUIS: I can't reach it!

LAUREEN: Bring it here. I'll pull it out.

PABLO: Stay where you are! All of you!

LOUIS: Even me?

PABLO: Especially you. We have to determine the exact angle of projectory. You'll mess everything up if you start moving around.

LOUIS: Call a doctor, Pablo. I'm not kidding. I've got an arrow stuck in my back.

PABLO: I can appreciate that but we can't have everyone moving around and destroying the evidence.

LOUIS: Call the Squad then. We need extra help! There's too many of them for us to handle. They're coming at us through the woodwork! I didn't even see it coming.

PABLO: We can handle it. We've been on tougher assignments than this. We've been to Cuba, Louis! You forget that! We've both been to Cuba and back.

LOUIS: No one's supposed to know about that.

PABLO: It's all right now. Now we can pull out all the stops.

LOUIS: Am I bleeding?

PABLO: It's a superficial abrasion. You'll pull through. I guarantee it. 'Intelligence' is a risky business. You knew that when you joined up.

LAUREEN: How did you two get in here anyway?

PABLO: I'll do the questioning sister, if you don't mind.

LAUREEN: Stop calling me sister. I'm not your sister.

PABLO: You're as fishy as a cat in heat lady.

LAUREEN: Very flattering.

PABLO: First you slink in here—you and your friend—and claim to be waiting for this Niles character to show up.

LAUREEN: That's right.

PABLO: And then you turn around and tell us to lay off the case because the guy's dead. Now which is it? Dead or alive? What's the story?

PETRONE: I was in the midst of telling you the whole story but you guys are hysterical.

PABLO: *(To* PETRONE*)* Just shut up until you're spoken to! My partner's been shot in case you haven't noticed. This whole thing has taken on a new dimension.

LAUREEN: That's what we're after.

PABLO: What?

LAUREEN: A new dimension. What's the point in messing around in the same old dimension all the time.

LOUIS: Because it's safe, that's why! You don't get shot in the back when you're not looking! You don't get sudden sweeping surges of terror coursing through your blood! You don't get the urge to end the whole thing right here and now!

LAUREEN: Yes you do but it just comes later. It comes at the end of your life instead of the middle.

LOUIS: I'm in my prime! I deserve better than this.

PABLO: Louis shut up! I can't hear myself think. *(Puts his fingers in his ears)*

LAUREEN: It comes when all your friends have died off and you're just laying there with the radio playing. Just going in circles. Same old thoughts, just repeating themselves. Over and over. It's too late then. All the doors are shut. But you can still hear your life going on. Somewhere outside. Somewhere way outside.

LOUIS: I'm not listening anymore. I can't take it! *(Puts his fingers in his ears)* LAUREEN *starts bowing bass as* PETRONE *mimes sax.* LAUREEN *speaks as she plays.* PABLO *and* LOUIS *keep their fingers in their ears as she speaks.*

LAUREEN: You struggle to the window. You hold yourself up by both elbows and stare down at the street, looking for your life. But all you see down there is yourself looking back up at you. You jump back from the window. You fall. You lay there gaping at the ceiling. You're pounding all over. You crawl back for another look. You can't resist. You pull yourself up to the window sill and peer down again. There you are, still standing down there on the street. Still looking straight back up at yourself. Your terror drops for a second. Long enough to start getting curious. You look hard at yourself on the street. You check out all the details. You examine yourself in a way you never have before. Not to resolve any conflicts but only to make an absolute identification. You check the face, the hands, the eyes, the turns in the mouth. You look for any sign that might give him away to you as an imposter. A man in disguise. But then you see him signaling to you from the street. He's pointing to his head, to his own head, then pointing back to you. He keeps repeating this over and over as though it's very important. As though it's something you should have understood a long, long time ago but never did. You pick up the gesture from him and start repeating it back to him. Pointing at your head first then pointing down to him on the street. He starts to nod his head and smiles as though you've finally got the message. But you're still not clear what he means. You pry open the window with the last strength you've got and the shock of cold air almost kills you on the spot. "If only I don't die before I find out what he means!"

You say. "Just let me live five minutes longer." Then you see him more clearly than before. You see for sure that he is you. That he's not pretending. He yells up to you in a voice you can't mistake. He yells at you so the whole street can hear him. "YOU'RE IN MY HEAD! YOU'RE ONLY IN MY HEAD!" Then he turns and walks away. You watch him go until you can't see him any more. Then you make a clean jump all the way to the bottom. And your life goes dancing out the window.

LAUREEN *stops playing the bass abruptly.* PABLO *and* LOUIS *take their fingers out of their ears. Lights go black on stage. Follow spots up on* NILES *and* PAULLETTE. NILES *dressed this time in black tails, puffing on cigar while* PAULLETTE *circles him again, checking out the fit of the costume.*

NILES: *(To* PAULLETTE*)* I'm not sure if I have the theory straight. I'm not even sure where the theory came from.

PAULLETTE: It came from you.

NILES: Are you sure? I remember having some ideas about all this and then you took it further. You found someone who knew about this stuff.

PAULLETTE: If you have visitors you don't want, you should get rid of them.

NILES: *(To himself)* Never give your address out to bad company.

PAULLETTE: What?

NILES: Nothing. I agree about getting rid of them but what I question is the means; the technique.

PAULLETTE: It's no technique. It's a ritual.

NILES: Yeah, but it seems so stupid. So primitive. I mean I'm not a kid. I know that if you dress up funny, like another person and then you pretend to shoot that person—

PAULLETTE: I wasn't pretending. I shot him.

NILES: Yeah, but I didn't die. I'm not even wounded. Look.

PAULLETTE: He died. That's the whole point. You don't want to kill yourself do you?

NILES: No. Yes. No.

PAULLETTE: Just these other ones.

NILES: Yeah, but I'm not really sure if there actually are these other ones or if I'm making it all up.

PAULLETTE: Doesn't matter.

NILES: Why not?

PAULLETTE: It's the same. They're the same thing.

NILES: That's crazy. You can't just invent someone and have them appear.

PAULLETTE: Sure you can. You did.

NILES: *(Suddenly terrified)* Is that the one we killed!

PAULLETTE *backs away from him.*

NILES: *(After pause)* Is that the one whose face we blew off! *(No answer from* PAULLETTE*)* Is it Paullette! WHOSE FACE DID WE BLOW OFF?

PAULLETTE: Somebody else's.

NILES: WHO WAS IT?

PAULLETTE: Look, we're messing with something that's very tricky. I can't help it if an accident sneaks in here and there.

NILES: I'll kill myself before I go to jail! I'm not going to jail, Paullette.

PAULLETTE: In this state they hang you.

NILES: I don't mind getting hung but I'm not going to jail.

PAULLETTE: You won't.

NILES: Was it someone important we killed?

PAULLETTE: Who knows.

NILES: You know!

PAULLETTE: I don't know everything. It was an experiment. It just so happened it worked. We fooled them. They took it as suicide. Clean and simple. Leave it at that.

NILES: It was someone important. I can remember his face now. The kind of face that looks over-fed. Too much rich food and not enough exercise. What was he doing here?

PAULLETTE: Knock it off, Niles! We can't back-track now. There's not enough time.

NILES: He was pleading with us. I remember him pleading. Chewing on his tie. It was cruel beyond belief.

PAULLETTE: Turn around and let's do the next one.

PAULLETTE *moves to the suitcase.*

NILES: He was miserable. He was surrounded by everything he ever wanted. What was he doing with us? Why us?

PAULLETTE: He knew we'd cooperate.

NILES: I remember what he said! I remember exactly what he said! He said, "look now at the state of things. Look closely at the state of things. You won't ever see it again exactly as it is now. This is it.

If you don't catch it now, it'll all be gone tomorrow. You have to look with a penetrating vision in order to catch it because everything lies in the name of the truth. Everything is trying to convince you it isn't what it is." Why did he say that?

PAULLETTE: He was lying.

She turns suddenly towards him with an automatic pistol which she's taken from the suitcase and fires a full round of ammunition into him. He just stands there. Stage lights up as spots go out. PABLO *staggers around the stage doubled over, holding his stomach.* PABLO *screams.*

PABLO: *(Staggering)* THEY GOT ME LOUIS! THIS TIME THEY REALLY GOT ME! I'M GUT SHOT! RIGHT THROUGH THE SMALL INTESTINE! CALL THE SQUAD! TELL THEM WE DID OUR BEST! WE ACTED BEYOND THE CALL OF DUTY! WE USED EVERY MEANS POSSIBLE TO COME TO TERMS WITH THE ENEMY! WE TRIED TO REASON! WE TRIED TO CONNIVE! BUT NOTHING WORKED! IN THE END WE WERE DEFEATED BY GHOSTS! AN UNSEEN ENEMY! IN THE END WE WERE NOT CERTAIN! WE COULD MAKE NEITHER HEAD NOR TAIL OF THE PRE-DICAMENT! WHETHER OR NOT WE WERE DESTROYED FROM WITHIN OR WITHOUT! NOW IT MAKES NO DIF-FERENCE! THERE IS ONLY THE REALITY OF MY DYING! TELL THEM THAT! WRITE IT DOWN! LOUIS! WRITE IT DOWN BEFORE YOU FORGET!

PABLO *falls to the floor on top of the outline. The others stand watching him lie there.* PABLO *gasps heavily as though going into a coma.*

LOUIS: *(To others, watching* PABLO*)* What did he say?

LAUREEN: *(Setting down the bass on the floor)* I couldn't make it out. *She crosses to the armchair and collapses into it.*

PETRONE: Too bad Niles didn't show. He would've liked this. Some-times it was hard for us to even get him to eat. He'd go for days just staring straight ahead of himself. I'd try to tell him it wasn't all that bad. Nothing's all that bad. I'd try to tell him the worst was imaginary. But it wouldn't penetrate. He'd just sit there and stare.

LAUREEN: *(In chair)* I'm exhausted.

PETRONE: I knew, ya' know, because I'd been there before. I could recognize his state. I could see it in his eyes. A kind of deadness. Like he'd died inside. Given up.

LOUIS: *(Still staring at* PABLO *on the floor)* Is there a telephone?

PETRONE: I'd been like that so I knew. The difference was that I went through it. Clear on through it. But he never made it. He had no idea that things would change. He took it to the end.

LOUIS: *(To* PETRONE*)* I've got to make contact with the outside world. Isn't there a phone somewhere?

LAUREEN: *(To* LOUIS*)* You're mistaken if you think it's different out there. It's just the same.

PETRONE: It's worse.

LAUREEN: It's just the same.

LOUIS: WHY ARE WE BEING SYSTEMATICALLY BUMPED OFF BY AN UNSEEN ENEMY! IT'S NOT FAIR!

LAUREEN: The planet is going crazy.

LOUIS: That's no explanation! I've got an arrow in my back and Pablo's been gut shot! Don't blame it on the planet!

PETRONE: I have a feeling you'll never get to the bottom of it. He never did. That's one thing he couldn't understand. The one thing that killed him.

PABLO: *(Still on floor, ear to floor, listening, gasping)* I can hear him breathing still, Louis. He's still with us! Still around! Check the next room! Check all the exits! We're not alone!

LOUIS: I'm paralyzed Pablo! I never thought it would be this tough.

LAUREEN: *(In chair)* He had that kind of quality. That kind of presence. He'd move into a room and everything would change.

PABLO: *(On floor)* He's after us, Louis! Right now he's after us! He thinks we're out to get him.

LOUIS: I never even met him!

PETRONE: I can remember him the very first time. Moving through the streets like a Kodiak bear. I followed him for blocks. An umbrella half hid him from behind but his shape was unmistakeable.

Spot comes up on NILES *down left walking slowly with* PAULLETTE *clinging onto his arm like a little girl.* NILES *carries a small black umbrella. They move silently across the stage as* PETRONE *narrates in half light. Piano music comes in softly.*

PETRONE: A small girl played at his sleeves like a puppy pulling at its mother's tits, trying to get a grip then falling back then trying again.

I was mesmerized by his progress. His immense size only added to the sense of awe. The entire city stood out around him like a miniature replica. A backdrop to his steady walking. Now and then he'd stop and buy a bag of green grapes which he'd share with the girl. It wasn't raining but he kept the umbrella perched on his shoulder as though he'd forgotten it was there.

LAUREEN: *(Still in chair)* That was Spring I remember. City Spring. The Mayor was negotiating with the street gangs to keep the city cool for the coming summer heat wave. His "men in Blue" were buying off the leaders with laundry bags of raw opium.

PETRONE: *(Moving slightly toward* NILES *downstage,* NILES *keeps talking with* PAULLETTE*)* That was it! The weather. The change in the season. The city change. Not like the country where you see it coming on gradual, bit by bit. Every day a slightly different color to the trees. A slow emerging. This was sudden. Abrupt. Bang. There it was. Now I connect it!

PABLO: *(on floor)* To what? Don't leave us whatever you do!

PETRONE: *(to* PABLO*)* To the feeling I was feeling. I didn't make the connection then but now it's clear. A raw despair.

LOUIS: With Spring? What age are we living in? Spring is full of promise! Spring has always been full of promise! Arrows can't change that! Terrorism can't change that!

LAUREEN: *(To* LOUIS*)* Pipe down, you dope. Have respect for a man's reveries.

PETRONE: *(Moving closer to* NILES, *watching him intensely,* NILES *pays no attention, just keeps walking)* The lateness of the day. The 'daylight savings time.' Still not dark at eight P.M.. Everything was adding up. Piling up. Brothers were jumping off apartment buildings into broad daylight. Sisters disappeared down elevator shafts. Methadone programs were taking their toll. Coltrane was gone. Dolphy was gone. But Niles was right there. Right there in front of me. Walking. Still moving. His music wrapped up and carried inside him. Protected. Hidden from all the pedestrians. I followed him closely. I watched his every move as though some magic would escape his gestures and plunge into me. As though his music would start playing from his skin and jump back to my skin, transforming me, changing me, filling me up. Taking away everything deadly. Taking all this awful, empty loneliness and making me whole again. Making me feel alive.

NILES *turns abruptly on* PETRONE *who's been following him closely.*
PAULLETTE *hides behind* NILES.

NILES: Are you following me? Is that it?

PETRONE: *(Stepping back)* Sorry. I didn't realize I was getting so close.

NILES: You're too close for comfort.

PETRONE: It was just that I recognized you and—

NILES: You recognized me? How could you recognize me when I don't even recognize myself?

PETRONE: I don't know. I've seen you play.

NILES: That was someone else.

NILES *turns sharply away from* PETRONE *and walks away with* PAUL-
LETTE *trying to hide behind him.* PETRONE *follows.*

PETRONE: No! It was you. You're so big I could never mistake you.

NILES *stops suddenly again and turns to* PETRONE.

NILES: Did you listen or just watch?

PETRONE: What do you mean?

NILES: Did you listen to the music!

PETRONE: Yeah. Sure.

NILES: What did it say?

PETRONE: What?

NILES: What did the music say? Did you hear it?

PETRONE: Yes. It wasn't words. I mean it wasn't words like we're talking now.

NILES: Of course not! What did it say?

PETRONE: It said that there was a chance.

NILES: What kind of chance?

PETRONE: A slim chance but still a chance.

NILES: And you'd given up hoping and this chance you heard filled you with hope and now that you've seen me on the street you think that just by coming in contact with me that your asslicking life will be saved from hopelessness.

PETRONE: Yes.

NILES: No chance.

NILES *turns again and walks away from him,* PETRONE *follows.*

PETRONE: Just saying that doesn't make any difference. It doesn't change it.

NILES: Get away from me! The sidewalk's not big enough for the three of us!

PETRONE: I know where you live Niles!

NILES *stops dead.* PETRONE *stops.* NILES *turns slowly toward* PE-
TRONE. PAULLETTE *trembles behind* NILES.

PAULLETTE: He's lying! He's working for any number of malevolent
organizations! You can see it in his eyeballs!

PETRONE: I know, Niles.

NILES: *(Moving slightly toward him)* What do you know?

PAULLETTE: This is a trick! I've seen it a million times! They sucker you.
They promise you! They "yes" you to death and then they slam you
in the "Tombs." Don't buy it Niles!

NILES: *(To* PETRONE*)* What do you know!

PETRONE: I know that you sold it all down the river. The whole fan-
dango.

NILES: Sold what?

PETRONE: I know that you were rewarded before your time. Before your
"coming of age." That you "bought it" from the big boys. You
swallowed it whole.

PAULLETTE: This is lying claptrap! I can recognize an evil force when
I see one!

NILES: *(To* PAULLETTE*)* Shut up!

PETRONE: I can take you home, Niles. Back to the scene of the crime.

NILES: What for? I'm safe now. I'm on the streets. Anonymous. Why
should I go back.

PETRONE: To clean house.

NILES: Who's there? Is there someone there in my house? Who is it!

PETRONE: I'll show you.

PAULLETTE: Don't follow him, Niles! He'll nail you for sure.

NILES: What're they doing there? Why can't they leave me alone?

PETRONE: *(Motioning to others upstage,* NILES *sees them)* Take a look.
They're crawling all over your furniture, across your floor, inside
your walls. Take a look Niles.

Lights up bright on upstage people

NILES: Get them out of there! I'm already dead! Don't they know that.
(Yelling at them upstage) I'M ALREADY DEAD!

PETRONE: Now's your chance, Niles. You can clean the slate. You've
got them all in one place at the same time. It's perfect. You can wipe
them all out.

NILES: *(To* PETRONE*)* What's your interest in this. What's in it for you?

PETRONE: I'm a fan. A fanatic. I live for revenge.

NILES: *(After short pause)* Take me inside.

NILES *follows* PETRONE *into the upstage area with the others.* PAUL-LETTE *follows them at a distance.*

PAULLETTE: Niles! It's a trap! It's worse than a trap! THEY'LL TEAR YOU APART NILES!

    PAULLETTE *watches* NILES *for a second then runs off stage right. The others watch* NILES *closely as he strolls through the space. Silence.*

NILES: What's happened to all of you?

LAUREEN: *(Still in chair)* We've been waiting.

NILES: For me?

LAUREEN: We've been waiting to play.

NILES: You don't need me for that.

LOUIS: *(To* PETRONE*)* Is this him?

PETRONE: This is him.

LOUIS: Alive?

PABLO: *(On floor)* I knew it! I knew it! I could hear him breathing!

NILES: *(To* PABLO*)* Get up off my floor. *(*PABLO *stands slowly)*

NILES: *(To* PABLO*)* Does everyone grovel in your profession?

PABLO: I wasn't groveling. I was on the verge of prayer.

NILES: Religious? Something drove you to get religious?

PABLO: It's my last hope.

NILES: *(Turning to* LOUIS*)* How about you? Religious?

LOUIS: I have no faith. I subscribe to no system of thought. I'm on the verge of total madness.

NILES: The verge. Only the verge?

LOUIS: What's the point in going further!

NILES: *(Turning to* PETRONE*)* What's the point, Petrone?

PETRONE: No point.

NILES: No point. *(Starts moving through space)* Petrone's been over the edge on several occasions and he confirms your suspicion. No point. Absolutely nothing to be gained by going off the deep end. Right, Laureen?

LAUREEN: Absolutely.

NILES: Laureen herself is a confirmed basket case and even she agrees. Madness sucks.

LOUIS: *(Bursting out)* I'm dedicated to the pursuit of truth at whatever cost! Where's the telephone!

NILES: What a position we're in. We've all lost our calling. How could that be?

PETRONE: We're ready to play, Niles. Just say the word.

NILES: There is no word to say. If you feel like playing go ahead.

PETRONE *picks up saxophone and begins playing silently again.*

NILES: What's everyone waiting for? Are you here to arrest me? Is that it? In my own house? Am I dead or alive? Is that it? Is this me here, now? Are these questions or answers? Are you waiting for the truth to roll out and lap your faces like a Bloodhound's tongue? Are you diving to the bottom of it? Getting to the core of the mystery? Getting closer? Moving in for the kill? Waiting for one wrong move when they're all wrong moves? Sifting through the reams of corruption? Toppling politicians in your wake?

LAUREEN *stands and starts bowing the bass in long mournfull notes. Piano fills softly behind.* LOUIS *and* PABLO *start to move in on* NILES *very slowly, almost unnoticed as he raves on.*

NILES: Are you martyring yourselves with your own criminal instincts? Are you inside me or outside me? Am I inside you? Am I inside you right now? Am I buzzing away at your membranes? Your brain waves? Driving you berserk? Creating explosions? Destroying your ancient patterns? Or am I just like you? Just exactely like you? So exactly like you that we're exactly the same. So exactly that we're not even apart. Not even separate. Not even two things but just one. Only one. Indivisible.

PABLO *and* LOUIS *arrive simultaneously on either side of* NILES *and snap hand cuffs on both of his wrists. The other half of each pair of hand cuffs is locked onto their own wrists so that all three are locked to each other.* NILES *makes no move of protest. The sound of the snapping hand cuffs should happen in a moment of silence between the language and the music.*

NILES: *(After short silence)* Someone was killed here for sure. I saw him face to face. I saw his whole life go past me. Someone should pay for that. That's for sure. Someone should be made to pay for that. A life's not cheap, that's for sure. You guys know that. You've seen enough to know that. You've been around. You've been through the war. You're nobody's fool. He had his whole face torn off. Beyond recognition. Right down to the bone. I think he was alive at the time. Right up to the last. He stayed alive right through it. Right up to the point where he died. He was alive to the very last moment. You know what that's like.

PABLO *and* LOUIS *lead* NILES *off stage right. Piano music swells along with sax and bass. Lights fade very slowly on* PETRONE, LAUREEN *and* PIANO PLAYER. *Lamp shade stays lit in dark then goes out.*

OTHER BOOKS OF INTEREST PUBLISHED BY URIZEN

LITERATURE

Bataille, Georges
Story of the Eye,
120 p. / Cloth $5.95

Bresson, Robert
Notes on Cinematography,
132 p. / $6.95 / paper $3.50

Brodsky, Michael
Detour, novel,
350 p. / Cloth $8.95

Cohen, Marvin
The Inconvenience of Living, fiction,
200 p. / Cloth $8.95 / paper $4.95

Ehrenburg, Ilya
The Life of the Automobile, novel,
192 p. / Cloth $8.95 / paper $4.95

Enzensberger, Hans Magnus
Mausoleum, poetry,
132 p. / Cloth $10.00 / paper $4.95

Hamburger, Michael
German Poetry 1910-1975,
576 p. / Cloth $17.50 / paper $7.95

Handke, Peter
Nonsense & Happiness, poetry,
80 p. / Cloth $7.95 / paper $3.95

Innerhofer, Franz
Beautiful Days, novel,
228 p. / Cloth $8.95 / paper $4.95

Kroetz, Franz Xavier
Farmyard & Other Plays,
192 p. / Cloth $12.95 / paper $4.95

Shepard, Sam
*Angel City, Curse of the Starving
   Class & Other Plays,*
300 p. / Cloth $15.00 / paper $4.95

MOLE EDITIONS

Clastres, Pierre
Society Against the State,
188 p. / Cloth $12.95

Elias, Norbert
The Civilizing Process, Vol. 1 & 2,
400 p. / Cloth $15.00 each Vol.

Gibson, Ian
The English Vice,
364 p. / Cloth $12.95

Schivelbusch, Wolfgang
The Railway Journey,
275 p. / photos / Cloth $15.00

Sternberger, Dolf
Preface by Erich Heller
Panorama of the 19th Century
212 p. / Cloth $15.00

ECONOMICS

DeBrunhoff, Suzanne
Marx on Money,
192 p. / Cloth $10.00 / paper $4.95

Howard, Dick
The Marxian Legacy,
340 p. / Cloth $15.00 / paper $5.95

Linder, Marc
Anti-Samuelson, Vol. I,
400 p. / Cloth $15.00 / paper $5.95
Anti-Samuelson, Vol. II,
440 p. / Cloth $15.00 / paper $5.95

CONTEMPORARY AFFAIRS

Andrew Arato / Eike Gebhardt (Eds.)
*The Essential Frankfurt School
   Reader,*
554 p. / Cloth $17.50 / paper $6.95

Augstein, Rudolf
Preface by Gore Vidal
Jesus, Son of Man,
420 p. / Cloth $12.95 / paper $4.95

Burchett, Wilfred
Southern Africa Stands Up,
Cloth 12.95 / paper $4.95

Kristeva, Julia
About Chinese Women,
250 p. / Cloth $8.95

Ledda, Galvino
Padre, Padrone,
Cloth $9.95

Sartre, Jean-Paul
Sartre by Himself,
136 p. / photos / Cloth $10.95 / paper $3.95

Steele, Jonathan
Inside East Germany,
300 p. / Cloth $12.95

Stern, August
The USSR vs. Dr. Mikhail Stern,
420 p. / Cloth $12.95

Write for a complete catalog and send orders to:
Urizen Books, Inc., 66 West Broadway, New York, N.Y. 10007
212 - 962-3413